GLOBALIZATION

We are surrounded by globalizing developments: the emergence of the global communications industry; the growth of multinational enterprises; the influence of global financial markets; global warming; and international action on human rights. These have brought the idea of a global society into prominence. We now recognise that the constraints of geography are shrinking and that the world is becoming a single place. In this crisp and incisive book, Malcolm Waters provides a much needed guide to the concept in social theory and the social, economic and political consequences.

The first two chapters offer a critical summary of the main theories of globalization, outlining the standard contributions – modernization and convergence, the capitalist world-system, transnationalization and the global village – before moving on to tease out the common threads in the contemporary globalization theories of Robertson, Giddens, Harvey and Beck.

The succeeding chapters trace the effects of the process through the arenas of economy, politics and culture. Here the book gives a lively treatment to such topics as planetary environmentalism, the new international division of labour, the new world order, growing religious fundamentalism and democratization and marketization. These topics are integrated within a theoretical account that views globalization as the consequence of the new pre-eminence of culture in social life.

Malcolm Waters is Professor of Sociology at the University of Tasmania, Australia.

KEY IDEAS
Series Editor: Peter Hamilton
The Open University

KEY IDEAS
Series Editor: PETER HAMILTON
The Open University, Milton Keynes

Designed to complement the successful *Key Sociologists*, this series covers the main concepts, issues, debates and controversies in sociology and the social sciences. The series aims to provide authoritative essays on central topics of social science, such as community, power, work, sexuality, inequality, benefits and ideology, class, family, etc. Books adopt a strong individual 'line' constituting original essays rather than literary surveys and form lively and original treatments of their subject matter. The books will be useful to students and teachers of sociology, political science, economics, psychology, philosophy and geography.

THE SYMBOLIC CONSTRUCTION OF COMMUNITY
ANTHONY P. COHEN, Department of Social Anthropology, University of Manchester

SOCIETY
DAVID FRISBY and DEREK SAYER, Department of Sociology, University of Manchester

SEXUALITY
JEFFREY WEEKS, Social Work Studies Department, University of Southampton

WORKING
GRAEME SALAMAN, Faculty of Social Sciences, The Open University, Milton Keynes

BELIEFS AND IDEOLOGY
KENNETH THOMPSON, Faculty of Social Sciences, The Open University, Milton Keynes

EQUALITY
BRYAN TURNER, School of Social Sciences, The Flinders University of South Australia

HEGEMONY
ROBERT BOCOCK, Faculty of Social Sciences, The Open University, Milton Keynes

RACISM
ROBERT MILES, Department of Sociology, University of Glasgow

POSTMODERNITY
BARRY SMART, Associate Professor of Sociology, University of Auckland, New Zealand

CLASS
STEPHEN EDGELL, School of Social Sciences, University of Salford

CONSUMPTION
ROBERT BOCOCK, Faculty of Social Sciences, The Open University, Milton Keynes

CULTURE
CHRIS JENKS, Department of Sociology, Goldsmiths' College

MASS MEDIA
PIERRE SORLIN, University of Paris III

GLOBALIZATION

MALCOLM WATERS

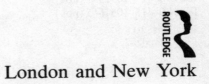

London and New York

First published 1995
by Routledge
11 New Fetter Lane, London EC4P 4EE

Simultaneously published in the USA and Canada
by Routledge
29 West 35th Street, New York, NY 10001

Reprinted 1996 (twice), 1998 (twice)

Typeset in Times by
Intype, London
Printed and bound in Great Britain by
Clays Ltd, St Ives plc

British Library Cataloguing in Publication Data
A catalogue record for this book is available from the British
Library

Library of Congress Cataloging in Publication Data
A catalog record for this book is available from the Library
of Congress

ISBN 0–415–10575–7 (hbk)
ISBN 0–415–10576–5 (pbk)

He had bought a large map representing the sea,
    Without the least vestige of land:
And the crew were much pleased when they found it to be
    A map they could all understand.

'What's the good of Mercator's North Poles and Equators,
    Tropics, Zones, and Meridian Lines?'
So the Bellman would cry: and the crew would reply,
    'They are merely conventional signs!

'Other maps are such shapes, with their islands and capes!
    But we've got our brave Captain to thank'
(So the crew would protest) 'that he's bought us the best –
    A perfect and absolute blank!'

The Hunting of the Snark Lewis Carroll

Contents

List of figures and tables

List of figures and tables

Preface

Although conceivably surpassed by Tierra del Fuego or Outer Mongolia, Tasmania's geographical location makes it just about the perfect place from which to assess the extent of globalization. If one can sit here at the spatial edge of human society, looking northward across the vast desert continent of Australia and southward towards emptiness and desolation, knowing that one is thousands of kilometres from the 'global cities' of Tokyo, Frankfurt, or LA, and still feel that one is part of the world, then globalization truly is an impressive process. Tasmanians know that they live on one planet because other people's aerosol sprays have caused a carcinogenic hole in the ozone layer over their heads, because their relatively high rate of unemployment is due to a slump in the international commodities markets, because their children are exposed to such edifying role models as Robocop and The Simpsons, because their university is infested by the managerialist cultures of strategic planning, staff appraisal and quality control, just like everyone else's, because British TV-star scientists may drop in for a week to save their environment for them, and because their Gay community may at long last be able to experience freedom of sexual expression because it has appealed to the human rights conventions of the United Nations. It has become a commonplace to argue that globalization and localization are Janus-faced aspects of the same process but in this little local society of less than half a million souls that truth comes home more fully than in most.

I would like to be able to say that this book took many grinding years to write and that it needed the support of armies of friends and colleagues. Actually, it was one of those fortunate projects that took on a life of its own so that the book almost wrote itself in a relatively short time. Nevertheless, some important thanks are due. Chris Rojek must have been 'thinking globally' when he passed through Hobart and commissioned the project. Martin Albrow, Routledge's reviewer for both the proposal and the manuscript, encouraged it from the outset. Rowena Stewart and Christina Parnell made the sort of skilful administrative contribution for which I have to thank them far too often. Scott Birchall and Robert Hall made sure that my attempt at political science was not entirely off the planet. My thanks also must go to my family: to my wife, Judith Homeshaw, an 'ex-pom' policy analyst who cheerfully responds to my jibes at her discipline with her own withering criticisms of mine; and to our children, Penny (currently on a Rotary International student exchange in Germany) and Tom (an adept at soccer, marketed here as 'the world game'), for keeping me up to date on developments in global popular culture, whether I want to be or not.

Malcolm Waters
Hobart, Tasmania

Abbreviations

<table>
<tr><td>AGIL</td><td>Adaptation/goal-attainment/integration/latent pattern-maintenance and tension management</td></tr>
<tr><td>APEC</td><td>Asia-Pacific Economic Council</td></tr>
<tr><td>ASEAN</td><td>Association of South-East Asian Nations</td></tr>
<tr><td>BINGO</td><td>Business international non-government organization</td></tr>
<tr><td>BT</td><td>British Telecom</td></tr>
<tr><td>CENTO</td><td>Central Treaty Organization</td></tr>
<tr><td>CFC</td><td>Chloro-fluoro carbon</td></tr>
<tr><td>CNN</td><td>Cable News Network</td></tr>
<tr><td>CPE</td><td>Centrally planned economy</td></tr>
<tr><td>DME</td><td>Democratic market economy</td></tr>
<tr><td>EC</td><td>European Community</td></tr>
<tr><td>ECSC</td><td>European Council for Security and Co-operation</td></tr>
<tr><td>EEC</td><td>European Economic Communities</td></tr>
<tr><td>EU</td><td>European Union</td></tr>
<tr><td>FAO</td><td>Food and Agriculture Organization of the United Nations</td></tr>
<tr><td>FDI</td><td>Foreign direct investment</td></tr>
<tr><td>G7</td><td>Group of seven leading industrial economies</td></tr>
</table>

GATT	General Agreement on Tariffs and Trade
GDP	Gross domestic product
IATA	International Air Transport Authority
IGO	International government organization
ILO	International Labour Organization
IMF	International Monetary Fund
INGO	International non-government organization
IPU	International Postal Union
IR	International Relations (academic discipline of)
ISA	International Sociological Association
ITU	International Telecommunications Union
JIT	Just-in-time production system
LDC	Less developed country
MAD	Mutually assured destruction
MDC	More developed country
MNC	Multinational corporation
MNE	Multinational enterprise
NAFTA	North American Free Trade Area
NATO	North Atlantic Treaty Organization
NIC	Newly industrializing country
NIDL	New international division of labour
NIEO	New International Economic Order
OECD	Organization for Economic Co-operation and Development
OED	*Oxford English Dictionary*
OPEC	Organization of Petroleum Exporting Countries
QCC	Quality control circle
SDR	Special drawing right
SEATO	South-East Asia Treaty Organization
TNC	Transnational corporation
UN	United Nations Organization
UNCTAD	United Nations Council for Trade and Development
UNESCO	United Nations Educational, Scientific and Cultural Organization
UNICEF	United Nations International Children's Emergency Fund
UNRRA	United Nations Relief and Rehabilitation Administration
WHO	World Health Organization
WTO	World Trade Organization
WWF	Worldwide Fund for Nature

1

A world of difference

Think global. Act local
Theodore Levitt

Social change is now proceeding so rapidly that if a sociologist had proposed as recently as ten years ago to write a book about globalization they would have had to overcome a wall of stony and bemused incomprehension. But now, just as postmodernism was *the* concept of the 1980s, globalization may be *the* concept of the 1990s, a key idea by which we understand the transition of human society into the third millenium. Curiously 'globalization' is far less controversial than 'postmodernism' (see Smart 1993). With the exception of the 'civilization analysts' that we shall mention in Chapter 3 most sociologists seem to accept that such a process is under way. Such controversies as there are appear to surround the issue of whether old Marxist or functionalist theories can be adapted to explain globalization or whether we need to construct novel arguments. This may be because sociological theories of change have almost always implied the universalization of the processes that they explain. Although it did not arise within sociology, the concept has therefore found instant appeal

across a range of intellectual interests. It remains for sociology
to connect the concept with its own vital theoretical traditions.
This short book seeks to contribute to this task.

Although the word 'global' is over 400 years old (*OED* 1989
s.v. global) the common usage of such words as 'globalization',
'globalize' and 'globalizing' did not begin until about 1960.[1] *The
Economist* (4/4/59) reported 'Italy's "globalised quota" for
imports of cars has increased'; and in 1961 *Webster* became the
first major dictionary to offer definitions of globalism and globalization. In 1962 *The Spectator* (5/10/62) recognized that: 'Globalisation is, indeed, a staggering concept'. (*OED* 1989 *s.v.* globalism,
globalization, globalize, globalized).

The concept certainly staggered or stumbled into academic
circles. Robertson (1992: 8) informs us that it was not recognized
as academically significant until the early or possibly the
mid–1980s but thereafter its use has become, well, globalized.
Although he says that its pattern of diffusion is virtually impposs-
ible to trace, it is beyond reasonable doubt that he is himself
centrally responsible for its currency in sociology. The many items
he has published on the topic include what is possibly the first
sociological article to include the word in its title (1985) although
he had used the concept of 'globality' somewhat earlier (1983).
Overall, the number of publications which use the word 'global'
in their titles has now probably reached five figures but the
processual term 'globalization' is still relatively rare. As at Febru-
ary 1994 the catalog of the Library of Congress contains only 34
items with that term or one of its derivatives in the title. None
of these was published before 1987.

The definitions of globalization given in general dictionaries
are often couched in such unhelpful terms as 'to render global'
or 'the act of globalizing'. Even if we delete the tautology as
in 'to render world-wide' or 'the act of diffusion throughout
the world' this is misleading from a sociological point of view
because it implies intentionality. Many aspects of globalization
are indeed intentional and reflexive including both the increasing
level of business planning for global marketing and action by the
environmentalist movement to save the planet. However many
globalizing forces are impersonal and beyond the control and
intentions of any individual or group of individuals. The development of Islamic fundamentalism as a response to the effects of
Western modernization or the decline of the American car industry are examples of just such effects.

Chapter 3 gives details of the various sociological definitions of globalization that seek to incorporate both the intentional and the non-intentional aspects of the process. However we need a working definition that will allow us to move forward to that analysis. Perhaps the best approach to such a definition might be to try to specify where the process of globalization might end, what a fully globalized world will look like. In a globalized world there will be a single society and culture occupying the planet. This society and culture will probably not be harmoniously integrated although it might conceivably be. Rather it will probably tend towards high levels of differentiation, multicentricity and chaos. There will be no central organizing government and no tight set of cultural preferences and prescriptions. Insofar as culture is unified it will be extremely abstract, expressing tolerance for diversity and individual choice. Importantly territoriality will disappear as an organizing principle for social and cultural life, it will be a society without borders and spatial boundaries. In a globalized world we will be unable to predict social practices and preferences on the basis of geographical location. Equally we can expect relationships between people in disparate locations to be formed as easily as relationships between people in proximate ones.[2]

We can therefore define globalization as: *A social process in which the constraints of geography on social and cultural arrangements recede and in which people become increasingly aware that they are receding.*

The concept of globalization is an obvious object for ideological suspicion because, like modernization, a predecessor and related concept, it appears to justify the spread of Western culture and of capitalist society by suggesting that there are forces operating beyond human control that are transforming the world. This book makes no attempt to hide the fact that the current phase of globalization is precisely associated with these developments. Globalization is the direct consequence of the expansion of European culture across the planet via settlement, colonization and cultural mimesis. It is also bound up intrinsically with the pattern of capitalist development as it has ramified through political and cultural arenas. However, it does not imply that every corner of the planet must become Westernized and capitalist but rather that every set of social arrangements must establish its position in relation to the capitalist West – to use Robertson's term, it must relativize itself. It must be said that in increasing sectors of the world this relativization process involves a positive preference for Western and capitalist possibilities. But globalization is also highly Europeanized in another sense. The de-territorialization of social and especially of political arrangements has proceeded most rapidly in the Western part of that continent – borders are becoming disemphasized and varieties of supra- and infranationalism are proliferating. This means that the model of globalization that is being globalized is itself a European model (i.e. developments within the EU are widely touted as the example for global de-territorialization; for example see Lash and Urry 1994: 281–3).

One of the theoretical debates about globalization surrounds when it began. As the review of theories in Chapter 3 will show, three possibilities can be specified:

- that globalization has been in process since the dawn of history, that it has increased in its effects since that time, but that there has been a sudden and recent acceleration;
- that globalization is cotemporal with modernization and the development of capitalism, and that there has been a recent acceleration; or
- that globalization is a recent phenomenon associated with other social processes called post-industrialization, post-modernization or the disorganization of capitalism.

The position taken in this book is that some measure of globalization has always occurred but that until about the middle of this millenium it was non-linear in its development. It proceeded through the fits and starts of various ancient imperial expansions, pillaging and trading oceanic explorations, and the spread of religious ideas. However the European middle ages, in particular, were a period of inward-looking territorialism that focused on locality, a slump in the globalization process. The linear extension of globalization that we are currently experiencing began in the fifteenth and sixteenth centuries, the 'early modern' period. Technically, and if one assumes that globalization is at least partly a reflexive process, globalization could not begin until that time because it was only the Copernican revolution that could convince humanity that it inhabited a globe. More importantly, until then the inhabitants of Eurasia-Africa, the Americas, and Australia lived in virtually complete ignorance of each other's existence. So the globalization process that is of most interest here is that associated with modernization.

GLOBALIZING SOLVENTS: THE CLASSICAL THEORIES

Curiously globalization, or a concept very much like it, put in an early appearance in the development of social science (Robertson 1992: 15–18; Turner 1990: 344–8). Saint-Simon (1975: 130–6) noticed that industrialization was inducing commonalities of practice across the disparate cultures of Europe. Seeking to hasten the process he argued for a utopian internationalism that included a pan-European government and a new and universalizing humanistic philosophy. These ideas were promoted through a publication presciently called *The Globe*. Saint-Simon's ideas found their way through Comte to Durkheim (1984) although the First World War led him to emphasize national rituals and patriotism. However, Durkheim's genuine legacy to globalization is his theories of differentiation and culture. To the extent that societies become structurally differentiated, commitment to such entities as the state must be weakened because they are more narrow in their compass. In parallel, the collective consciousness must progressively become more weak and abstract in order to encompass intra-societal diversity. All of this implies that industrialization tends to weaken collective commitments and to open the way for dismantling the boundaries between societies.

A similar comment might be made about Weber's (1978) contribution except that he was even more bound up than was Durkheim in his own national politics. Just as Durkheim identified differentiation, Weber identified rationalization as the globalizing solvent. He was fundamentally concerned with the success of rationalization, with its spread from the seed-bed origins of Calvinistic Protestantism to infest all Western cultures and to set up an 'iron cage' for all moderns. Rationalization implies that all cultures will become characterized by: 'the depersonalization of social relationships, the refinement of techniques of calculation, the enhancement of the importance of specialized knowledge, and the extension of technically rational control over both natural and social processes' (Brubaker 1984: 2). Although Weber did not recognize it, this implies a homogenization of cultures as well as that reduced commitment to such values as patriotism and duty of which he was aware. But even this globalizing effect was restricted to Western Europe. Weber saw no prospect of the spread of rationalized cultural preferences to say India or China which he regarded as inevitably mired in religious traditionalism.

Of all classical theorists, the one most explicitly committed to a globalizing theory of modernization is Marx. Globalization caused an enormous increase in the power of the capitalist class because it opened up new markets for it. Indeed the discovery of America and the opening of navigation routes to Asia established a 'world-market' for modern industry (Marx 1977: 222–3). The bourgeoisie rushed into this opportunity with alacrity: 'The need of a constantly expanding market for its products, chases the bourgeoisie over the whole surface of the globe. It must nestle everywhere, settle everywhere, establish connections everywhere'. (1977: 224). But this development is cultural as well as economic, Marx argues, because it gives a cosmopolitan character not only to production but to consumption:

> [National industries] are dislodged by new industries . . . that no longer work up indigenous raw material, but raw material drawn from the remotest zones; industries whose products are consumed, not only at home, but in every quarter of the globe. In place of the old wants, satisfied by the productions of the country, we find new wants, requiring for their satisfaction the products of distant lands and climes. In place of the old local and national seclusion and self-sufficiency, we have intercourse in every direction, universal interdependence of nations. And as in material, so also in intellectual production. The intellectual creations of individual nations become common property. National one-sidedness and narrow-mindedness become more and more impossible, and from the numerous national and local literatures, there arises a world literature.
>
> (1977: 224–5)

Nor is this process restricted to Western Europe. The bourgeoisie draws even 'barbarian' nations into its 'civilization' using the 'heavy artillery' of cheap commodities to batter down 'all Chinese walls'. The bourgeoisie is, for Marx, recreating the world in its own image.

However, notice that territorial boundaries remain. Marx refers to the interdependence of nations and recognizes the continuing existence of the nation-state. There is a seed of destruction, however, even for this. In establishing itself as a world capitalist class the bourgeoisie also causes the world proletariat to coalesce in opposition. The rise to power of the proletariat will, he argues, destroy all bourgeois institutions including the nation-state:

> National differences and antagonisms between peoples are daily more and more vanishing, owing to the development of the bourgeoisie, to freedom of commerce, to the world-market, to uniformity in the mode of production and in the conditions of life corresponding thereto.
>
> The supremacy of the proletariat will cause them to vanish still faster. United action, of the leading civilized countries at least, is one of the first conditions for the emancipation of the proletariat.
>
> In proportion as the exploitation of one individual by another is put an end to, the exploitation of one nation by another will also be put an end to. In proportion as the antagonism between classes within the nation vanishes, the hostility of one nation to another will come to an end.
>
> (1977: 235–6)

Although Marx's utopian vision of globalization might be regarded as romantic and unrealistic as Saint-Simon's the discussion of the link between capitalist production and a global consumer culture has remained highly influential.

A GUIDING THEOREM

Although the next two chapters of this book are addressed to recent theories of globalization that draw upon these classically established themes of change its main concern is to chart its substantive development. This section lays out the theoretical assumptions that underpin the argument.

Globalization is traced through three arenas of social life that have come to be recognized as fundamental in many theoretical analyses.[3] They are:

1 The economy: social arrangements for the production, exchange, distribution and consumption of goods and tangible services.
2 The polity: social arrangements for the concentration and application of power, especially insofar as it involves the organized exchange of coercion and surveillance (military, police etc.), as well as such institutionalized transform-

ations of these practices as authority and diplomacy, that can establish control over populations and territories.

3 Culture: social arrangements for the production, exchange and expression of symbols that represent facts, affects, meanings, beliefs, preferences, tastes and values.

Following Weber (1978: 928–40) and Bell (1979: 3–30), the argument takes these three arenas to be structurally independent. It therefore rejects both the Marxist position that the economy is constitutive of polity and culture and the Parsonsian position that culture determines the other two arenas. However, it also makes the assumption that the relative effectivity of the arenas can vary across history and geography. A more effective set of arrangements in one arena can penetrate and modify arrangements in the others. A concrete example can illustrate the point. For most of the twentieth century Russia and its adjacent territories and populations were controlled by the highly organized Soviet state, an effective polity. Here the state organized culture, allowing only certain forms of artistic expression and religious commitment, and it also organized the economy in a command system of state factories, farms, banks and shops. Here we can speak of the culture and the economy as having been politicized.

We can now start to link these themes into an argument about globalization. The claims of the theory of globalization centre on the relationship between social organization and territoriality. The proposal that drives the argument of this book is that this link is established by the types of exchange that predominate in social relationships at any particular moment. Different types of exchange apply to each of the arenas indicated above. Respectively they are:

- material exchanges including trade, tenancy, wage-labour, fee-for-service, and capital accumulation;
- political exchanges of support, security, coercion, authority, force, surveillance, legitimacy and obedience;
- symbolic exchanges by means of oral communication, publication, performance, teaching, oratory, ritual, display, entertainment, propaganda, advertisement, public demonstration, data accumulation and transfer, exhibition and spectacle.

Each of these types of exchange exhibits a particular relationship to space, respectively:

- Material exchanges tend to tie social relationships to localities: the production of exchangeable items involves local concentrations of labour, capital and raw materials; commodities are costly to transport which mitigates against long-distance trade unless there are significant cost advantages; wage-labour involves face-to-face supervision; service delivery is also most often face-to-face. Material exchanges are therefore rooted in localized markets, factories, offices and shops. Long-distance trade is carried out by specialist intermediaries (merchants, sailors, financiers, etc.) who stand outside the central relationships of the economy.

- Political exchanges tend to tie relationships to extended territories. They are specifically directed towards controlling the population that occupies a territory and harnessing its resources in the direction of territorial integrity or expansion. Political exchanges therefore culminate in the establishment of territorial boundaries that are coterminous with nation-state-societies. The exchanges between these units, known as international relations (i.e. war and diplomacy), tend to confirm their territorial sovereignty.

- Symbolic exchanges liberate relationships from spatial referents. Symbols can be produced anywhere and at any time and there are relatively few resource constraints on their production and reproduction. Moreover they are easily transportable. Importantly, because they frequently seek to appeal to human fundamentals they can often claim universal significance.

In summary then, the theorem that guides the argument of this book is that: *material exchanges localize; political exchanges internationalize; and symbolic exchanges globalize*. It follows that the globalization of human society is contingent on the extent to which cultural arrangements are effective relative to economic and political arrangements. We can expect the economy and the polity to be globalized to the extent that they are culturalized, that is, to the extent that the exchanges that take place within them are accomplished symbolically. We would also expect that the degree of globalization is greater in the cultural arena than either of the other two.

This is a radical proposal because it stands opposed to one of the most influential theories of global integration, Wallerstein's theory of the capitalist world-system (See Chapter 2), that takes its lead from Marx in suggesting that the driving force for global integration is restless capitalist expansionism. The view taken here is that the ability of purely material exchanges to move beyond a local nexus hit its limit towards the end of the nineteenth century at which point they were transformed into political exchanges (e.g. state colonial expansionism, alliance systems, global war, superpower arrangements). A similar transformation of political into symbolic exchanges is occurring at the present historical moment.

The next two chapters review sociological arguments about these processes. The first concentrates on post-war theories of global integration but which do not identify globalization as a unified process, the second focuses on explicit theories of globalization. Thereafter, the following three chapters review substantive globalizing developments in the economy, the polity and culture respectively.

2

What on earth is happening? Precursor theories

*There can be an awareness of world changes
without an awareness of that awareness.*
Fred Emery and Eric Trist

Macrosociology, the study of general social processes, usually takes 'society' as its unit of analysis. Insofar as macrosociology is concerned with modern society it must therefore focus on the nation-state. This is because, under modern conditions, society and the nation-state tend to be coterminous (Giddens 1985). Sociological theories of change have therefore always focused principally on the ways in which such general processes as rationalization or structural differentiation or class conflict affect the social structures of national societies. In what now appears to be tunnel vision, this orientation often went as far as making claims for the establishment of national sociologies, especially in cases where a national culture was under threat of invasion by a neighbouring one, or where two or more national cultures nestled unhappily within the bosom of a single state.

Nevertheless the reality of progressive global unification has always to some extent impressed itself on sociological macroanalysis. There are two main ways in which this impression has been made. First, more than many other social scientists, sociologists have been adept at noticing and analysing non-political relationships between societies. They have been particularly interested, for example, in the development of international monopoly capitalism and in its ability to transcend state boundaries. They have also been interested in international cultural diffusion especially within the medium of patterns of mass consumption and the spread of mass-mediated popular cultures. While other eyes have been resolutely focused on the nation-state as the organizing principle of modern society, the eyes of sociologists occasionally have wandered. Second, sociologists analysing social change have always had a natural tendency to construct grand explanatory schemes that will account for the broad sweep of history. Grand explanations always identify a single transformative principle and such principles must necessarily be understood as universalizing processes that break down boundaries and differences. Such a principle can be viewed as a penetrating solvent that will disrupt the peculiarities of national cultures and liberate populations so that they can have a free ride on the juggernaut of history, although always, of course with their backs to the engine.[1] Already we have mentioned, in the introduction to this book, three such solvents, Marx's capitalist commodification, Weber's rationalization, and Durkheim's differentiation.

In this chapter we consider some of the most important recent developments of this second type of theory. We consider first the thesis proposed largely in American functionalist social science that in a modernizing world, each society is likely to converge on a single set of axial principles for its social organization. On this argument each society moves towards a common social condition on the basis of choices rationally made by its members in relation to individual and collective advancement. The arguments we consider next, broadly derived from the work of Marx and Lenin, stand opposed to this position. They argue that the world is becoming unified not by choice but because of the domination of a single way of producing commodities, the capitalist mode of production. This system is so effective that it confers very high levels of social power on those who control production. Capitalists will use this power in order further to impose the capitalist system on (social and geographical) regions not previously included in its orbit. We then consider theories emerging from the International Relations branch of political science that suggest that a web of transnational connections is growing up alongside inter-state connections. Last, we examine what are perhaps the most promising of early perspectives on the globalization process, those that suggest that the world is being unified by the contagion of a common mass culture.

MODERNIZATION AND CONVERGENCE

In the introduction to this book we note that Durkheim had argued that the general direction of change in society was indicated by the process of structural differentiation. In the middle of the twentieth century, structural-functionalist sociologists expanded and modified Durkheim's argument to encompass the globalizing effects of differentiation. In thematic terms their thesis ran as follows. Industrialization involves a primary differentiation of capitalization and collective production from domestic production and reproduction. To the extent that a society can make this separation its material wealth and therefore its political success relative to other societies will increase. Once the option of industrialization is available political and economic leaders will therefore tend to choose and pursue it. Therefore industrialization spreads from its seedbed out into societal contexts in which it is not indigenous and the world becomes more industrialized. However, industrialization carries with it more general societal ramifications. It induces the pattern of differentiation to other areas of social life as these areas increasingly become functionally articulated with the industrial core – families specialize in consumption, schools teach differentiated skills to the labour force, specialized units of government provide economic infrastructure, the mass media sell appropriate symbolizations, churches promulgate supporting values, and so on. These structural changes induce value shifts in the direction of individualization, universalism, secularity and rationalization. This general complex of transformations is called 'modernization'. As industrialization spreads across the globe, it carries modernization with it, transforming societies in a unitary direction. Imitating societies may even adopt modern institutions before effectively industrializing.[2]

Parsons (1964; 1966) takes the lead in arguing that social change has a specific evolutionary direction and a logic or dynamic which drives it in this direction. The logic or dynamic is adaptation: 'the capacity of a living system to cope with its environment' (1964: 340). Modernization, theorized as differentiation, proceeds in the direction of adaptive upgrading:

> If differentiation is to yield a balanced, more evolved system, each newly differentiated sub-structure ... must have increased adaptive capacity for performing its primary function, as compared with the performance of that function in the previous, more diffuse structure. Thus economic production is typically more efficient in factories than in households.
>
> (Parsons 1966: 22)

This pattern is associated with two other developments (Parsons 1966: 22–3). The first is the Durkheimian process of integration. Differentiation forces an upgrading of the level of integration. Because differentiated social units are less self-sufficient and must make exchanges, social resources (human talent, knowledge, skills, capital, commodities, etc.) must become generalized and interchangeable. They are translated into the token forms of, for example, credentials, wages and salaries, and shares. This increased interchangeability provides a basis for the inclusion of out-groups within full and 'real' social membership. Modernization therefore breaks down status barriers (e.g. of social standing, ethnicity or gender) in particular and participation tends increasingly to become based on individual talent, merit and performance. The second development is in the arena of the general value-pattern of the society. The value-pattern must become both more complex, so that specific elements of it can be applied to differentiated sub-units, and more generalized, so as to legitimate the variety of goals and activities found in the upgraded social system. The value system of modern society therefore tends towards universalism and abstraction, so that it too is more inclusive. Each of these patterns of inclusion has clear implications for globalizing trends.

The institutional path which adaptive upgrading forces on any society can be traced through a series of 'evolutionary universals' (Parsons 1964), a concept based on the idea of natural selection in organisms. They are defined as: 'any organizational development sufficiently important to further evolution that, rather than emerging only once, it is likely to be 'hit upon' by various systems operating under different conditions' (1964: 329). Parsons identifies four base universals found in all, even the most undifferentiated of societies: technology, kinship, language, and religion.

Then there are two universals associated with evolution to the stage which Parsons calls intermediate societies (e.g. the ancient empires, feudalism). These are stratification and explicit cultural legitimation (written preservation of tradition). A further four universals are associated with the emergence of modern societies: bureaucratic organization, money and markets, a universalistic legal system and democratic association (both governmental and private). The key breakthrough from intermediate to modern society is an industrial production system based on individualized employment contracts and occupational specialization. This in turn sets up tensions of co-ordination and control and of commitment which induce the emergence of markets, bureaucracy and democracy.[3]

The implication of Parsons' analysis for globalization is simply that, if societies are driven along a common evolutionary path, they will become more alike and they will become more integrated along the lines of mechanical solidarity. A much more explicit link between modernization and the inter-societal system is developed by Parsons' student, Levy. Levy effectively reduces modernization to industrialization by defining it in the following way: 'A society will be considered more or less modernized to the extent that its members use inanimate sources of power and/ or use tools to multiply the effects of their efforts' (1966: 11). However, he also lists the major social-structural characteristics of a relatively modernized society (1966: 38–79). Many of these bear a close resemblance to Parsons' evolutionary universals:

- the units of society, its collectivities and roles, are highly specialized with respect to the type of activity which they perform; this means that individuals can specialize in the skills which they use in role performance;
- the units of society have a relatively low level of self-sufficiency – they must rely on other units to provide resources which they do not themselves produce;
- value-orientations are highly universalistic – they tend to stress what a person can do that is relevant to the situation rather than what they are;
- an increasing centralization of decision-making is set up by the need to coordinate and control diverse, specialized activities;
- a large proportion of human relationships are characterized

    by rationality, universalism, functional specificity and emotional avoidance;
- a large proportion of the exchanges between specialized units takes place by means of generalized media (e.g. money) and within market contexts;
- a widespread institutionalization of bureaucracy occurs, without which the coordination and control of specialized activities would be impossible; and
- the multilineal, conjugal family is established which covers a maximum of two generations, disemphasizes unilineal descent, and focuses on the spouse relationship as the foundational bond.

Here, however, Levy parts company with Parsons. The driving force behind modernization is no longer the impersonal functional imperative of adaptive upgrading but rather a materialistic motivation at the level of the individual agent. In societies that modernize early: 'no society has members completely unable to comprehend or sense advantages in some applications of power from inanimate sources and tools' (Levy 1966: 25–6). And latecomers are highly vulnerable to the 'universal social solvent' of modernization. Likewise, once a traditional society is in contact with a modernized society, at least some its members will want to change it in order to improve their material situation, more or less out of envy of the 'inordinate material productivity' of modern societies (1966: 125–6). The most imitated society becomes easy to specify: 'United States society . . . is the most extreme example of modernization' (1966: 36).

    Levy's argument, although frequently unrecognized within contemporary sociology, is significant within the conceptualization of globalization because he is able to show that latecomer modernization is essentially reflexive and that this reflexivity establishes a systemic pattern of inter-relationships between societies. For Levy the members of every society on the planet are faced by two questions, each of which presupposes that every society will indeed modernize: whether the modernization of non-modernized societies can be achieved in a stable (i.e. non-violent) fashion; and whether highly modernized societies can maintain their high rate of modernization as a stable condition. The first of these is not of absolute planetary significance but the second is: 'If those instabilities exist, they will spread with massive effects for all other individuals on the planet given the levels of interdependence already characteristic of the members of the different societies of the world' (1966: 790). For Levy then, modernization becomes a central problem-focus that phenomenologically unites the members of all societies.

However, the most influential functionalist precursor to globalization theory came not from any sociologist but from a group of Californian labour market theorists (Kerr *et al.* 1973). Kerr, Dunlop, Harbison and Myers propose a thesis of convergence between societies that has two strands. First they suggest that industrial societies are more similar to each other than to any non-industrial society. Second, although the industrialization process may be generated in different ways in different societies, industrial societies will over time become increasingly similar to one another. The driving force for this convergence is the 'logic of industrialism' – as societies progressively seek the most effective technology of production their social systems will also progressively adapt to that technology. Technological development will more closely determine some social relations than others, particularly the economic arenas of employment and consumption. However technology will necessarily ramify into most areas of social life.

Kerr *et al.* outline the key features of this societal convergence. The social division of labour advances insofar as individual skills become highly specialized so that the labour force becomes highly differentiated into occupations. As science and technology advance the occupational system will change inducing high rates occupational mobility. This process will be underpinned by very high levels of educational provision and credentialization. Equally industrial technology demands large-scale social organization in order to support mass production and mass marketing. Industrial societies will therefore be organized spatially into cities; governments will expand to provide a socialized infrastructure for industry; and organizations will generally be large in scale, hierarchical and bureaucratic. Industrial societies will also develop a distinctive value-consensus focused on materialism, commitment to work, pluralism, individual achievement, and progress for its own sake. They conclude that: 'The industrial society is world-wide' because: 'The science and technology on which it is based speak in a universal language' (1973: 54).

By the beginning of the third quarter of the twentieth century it was clear that these materialistic or technological arguments could not substantively be supported. There was an increasing recognition that culture could not be reduced to economic or class relationships. Indeed, by this time most occupational activity was not directed to the production of material commodities and did not employ machine technology. However, there was one last attempt to: 're-write the last chapter of [Durkheim's] *The Division of Labour* with a happy ending', as Archer (1990: 101) puts it. This is Bell's (1976) forecast of the emergence of 'post-industrial' society. In caricature, Bell specifies the post-industrial society as a game between people rather than a game between people and things. Its central characteristics are as follows:

- the number of people engaged in occupations producing services predominates over the number engaged in producing raw materials or manufactured goods; these occupations are predominantly professional and technical in character;
- the class structure changes in the direction of a system of statuses; the predominant status consists of members of professional and technical occupations; the locus of power shifts from the economic to the political sphere;
- theoretical knowledge predominates over practical knowledge and becomes the main source of innovation and policy formulation;
- technological development comes within the ambit of human control and planning; technological goals can be set and activities co-ordinated to accomplish them; invention is no longer an individualized activity governed by chance; and
- the most important technology is no longer physical but intellectual, so that human decisions previously based on intuitions and judgements can now be based on rational calculations within formulae.

However, the fundamentals of the argument are not too different from the convergence thesis. Kerr *et al.* (1973) argue that technologies for the production of goods create similarities between societies; Bell (1976) argues that emerging intellectual technologies for the production of services create that convergence. In Bell the emerging society is governed by a single axial principle (the use of theoretical knowledge to produce services) and it is specified as the only possible principle of future social organization. Therefore, all the societies on the planet march resolutely forward to a singular post-industrial future.

Bell's only explicit statement on globalization is contained in a short article (1987) that aims to forecast the future of the USA and the world in the years to 2013. Here he foreshadows some of the arguments reviewed in the subsequent chapters of this book. For example, he forecasts the elimination of geography as a 'controlling variable'. Markets can increasingly consist of electronically integrated networks and indeed employees will need less to be concentrated in a single place of work. The international economy will therefore be tied together in real time rather than in space. He also forecasts the disappearance of the nation-state. The evidence for this is the increasing internal fragmentation of states along national lines (Bell 1987: 13–14). They are fragmenting, he argues, because nation-states are inadequate to problems of global economic growth, third-world modernization, and environmental degradation, and are equally unresponsive and distant relative to the diversity of local needs and aspirations. However, it needs to be stressed that Bell's is not a fully fledged globalization thesis because it offers statements neither on the emergence of a phenomenology or culture of globalism nor on the systemic character of global social structure. Indeed, it is altogether pessimistic about the fragmentation of inter-state politics and the disruptive threats of population growth.

WORLD CAPITALISM

The view that globalization proceeds along a continuum of modernization dominated social scientific thought on global development in the thirty or so years after the Second World War. An appropriate metaphor for this view is that of countries as a series of mountain climbers clawing their way up 'Mount Progress'.[4] The strongest are near the top while others lag behind hampered by smallness of stature, poor equipment or lack of training. They meet blockages on their paths and cannot easily withstand natural calamities visited on them by landslide and climatic inclemency which occasionally throw them further down the mountain. The climbers near the top will often throw down ropes to haul the others up. Frequently the ropes are not strong enough because the good climbers never throw down their best ropes and are always selective about which of those lower down will receive help. However, most of the stragglers believe that by following in the footsteps of the lead climber they will all get there in the end. There are those who select an alternative route and refuse help from the lead climber but they are not doing nearly as well. When everyone gets to the summit they will join hands in mutual congratulation because they are all in the same place.

There has always been a problem in describing countries with differing positions in this developmental ascent. In the 1960s there were 'developed' and 'underdeveloped' countries; in the 1970s the 'first world' and the 'third world', with the 'second world', the state-socialist societies poised awkwardly between them; in the 1980s we spoke of 'more developed' and 'less developed' countries (MDCs and LDCs); and today of industrialized and newly industrializing countries (NICs). All of these indicate bipolarity in development terms, but more seriously, they imply that the origins of lower levels of development reside in the internal structure of a society. More recently, consideration of late industrialization has turned to the view that late and low industrializers are confirmed in that position by the relationships between themselves and the early industrializers. Insofar as inter-societal stratification is confirmed by such relationships we can affirm the existence of a single global system.

The origin of this argument about inter-societal stratification can be found in the work of the Bolshevik revolutionary, Lenin (1939). In his analysis of imperialism as the last or highest stage of capitalism Lenin argues that an international system of exploitation develops out of the social relations of capitalist production. The path of capitalist development which gives rise to this formation leads in the following direction. The earliest phase of capitalism is highly competitive as emerging capitalists seek to maximize profit at the expense of others. However, as some become more successful, and as the rate of profit falls, unevenness between firms in the capitalist market leads to the monopolization of its sectors as companies are forced out or absorbed by their more successful competitors. Monopolization allows price control, thus increasing the valorization of capital, which means that accumulated capital, rather than being re-invested, can be stored in a highly fluid and mobile form in banks. A finance-capital oligarchy emerges out of an institutional amalgamation between bank capital and industrial capital. This provides the mechanism for an extension of capitalist exploitation beyond national boundaries by means of capital exports. International capitalist monopolies form, dividing the world between themselves both economically and, through the agency of the colonial state, territorially.

Lenin specifies some important internal consequences for imperial societies. First, imperialism restructures the working class. Anticipating embourgeoisement arguments, Lenin makes a systematic distinction between the upper stratum of affluent workers and the lower stratum of the proletariat proper (1939: 105), the former enriched by overseas exploitation, the latter increased by immigration from the colonies. Imperialism therefore divides the workers, encourages individual opportunism and causes a 'temporary' decay of working-class movements, which can help to explain the postponement of socialist revolution.

We can now concentrate on two sympathetic refinements of Lenin's thesis. If we take that argument to its extreme, capital exports will eventually result in high, if uneven, levels of development in all parts of the world, assuming that the capitalist system has not collapsed under the force of its own Marxian logic. However, this widespread level of development plainly has not occurred. Monopoly-capitalist imperialism has indeed survived with considerable stability for about a century, but the reason, argues Frank (1971; Cockroft *et al.* 1972), is that monopolistic firms only give the appearance of being capital exporters when they are in fact net capital importers. They import profits made in the colonies which provide for internal capital accumulation. Capital exports to economic colonies are only 'seed money' investments, principally directed to the exploitation of labour for the production of food and raw materials. Colonial commodities can be imported to the centre at low prices while manufactured goods can be exported at high prices with the difference providing a surplus which returns to the investor and thus valorizes capital. As a consequence underdevelopment is perpetuated as a pattern of dependency between the colonialist and the colonized. Capital exports do not provide for the satellite development of industrial capitalism but only for a mercantile capitalism and thus a dependent and comprador[5] but nevertheless exploitative colonial bourgeoisie.

This globalizing effect is produced primarily because it is functional for the maintenance of capitalism at the centre. The enrichment process it provides gives rise to what Amin (1980: 26), in a Gramscian formulation, calls a 'social-democratic alliance'.

Like Lenin, Amin says that the industrial working class is divided
into two sectors, the first integrated and relatively privileged and
the second segmented and composed of disprivileged ethnic
minorities, women and young people. The social-democratic
alliance links the central bourgeoisie to the affluent working class
on one hand and to the satellite (comprador) bourgeoisie on
the other. By acting together these three groups can maintain the
status quo.

> Two main strategies, dictated by the international division
> of labor, are used to control the workforce: the repro-
> duction of the growing reserve army in the periphery,
> and the division of the working class in the center. . . .
> National and international monetary and credit policies
> (such as those of the International Monetary Fund)
> reinforce this dual control over the labor force and the
> international division of labor.
>
> (Amin 1980: 27)

Amin specifies the final stage of imperialist development as the
immiseration of the colonial proletariat and peasantry. Capitalist
exploitation monetarizes the colonial economy, thus providing a
potential market for consumer durables produced in the colonizing society. Subsistence agriculture cannot accommodate such a
market so it is replaced by a cash-crop agriculture which can.
The very development of cash-crop agriculture converts it into
an extension of capitalism. Small farmers are weak and dependent
on first-world prices, so their incomes progressively reduce, and
they eventually fail. Only a large-scale mechanized agriculture
can survive and this drives peasants off their land, contributes
to massive urbanization, urban unemployment and a significant
lumpenproletariat in the colonial or ex-colonial periphery.

The most influential sociological argument for considering
the world as a single economic system comes from Wallerstein
(1974; 1980; Hopkins and Wallerstein 1980; 1982). His primary
unit of analysis is the world-system, a unit which has a capacity
to develop independently of the social processes and relationships
which are internal to its component societies or states. A world-
system has the following chararcteristics (Wallerstein 1974:
347–8):

- the dynamics of its development are largely internal, that

is, they are not determined by events which occur outside it;
- it is materially self-contained and self-sufficient because
  it has an extensive division of labour between its component societies; and
- it contains a multiplicity of cultures which, when taken
  together, are viewed by individual participants as constituting 'the world' in a phenomenological sense.

There are three possible types of world-system:

- World-empires, in which a multiplicity of cultures are unified under the domination of a single government; there
  have been many instances of world-empires (e.g. ancient
  Egypt, ancient Rome, ancient China, Moghul India, feudal
  Russia, Ottoman Turkey).
- World-economies, in which a multiplicity of political states,
  each typically focusing on a single culture ('nation-states'),
  are integrated by a common economic system; there has
  been only one stable instance of a world-economy, the
  modern world-system, integrated by a single capitalist
  economy (which includes state socialist societies).
- World-socialism, in which both the nation-state and
  capitalism disappear in favour of a single, unified political-
  economic system which integrates a multiplicity of cultures;
  there is no instance of world-socialism and it remains a
  utopian construct.

Wallerstein concentrates on the emergence and evolution of the
modern, European world-system which he traces from its late
medieval origins to the present day. He describes the emergent
phenomenon in the following way:

> In the late fifteenth and early sixteenth century, there
> came into existence what we may call a European world-
> economy. It was not an empire yet but it was as spacious
> as an empire and shared some features with it. . . . It is a
> 'world' system, not because it encompasses the whole
> world, but because it is larger than any juridically-defined
> political unit. And it is a 'world-*economy*' because the
> basic linkage between the parts of the system is economic,
> although this was reinforced to some extent by cultural

links and eventually ... by political arrangements and
even confederal structures.

(Wallerstein 1974: 15; original italics)

A critical feature of Wallerstein's argument that differentiates it
from the dependency theory of Frank (1971) and Amin (1980) is
that the focal point of pressure in the world-economy is the state
structure. The state helps to stabilize capitalism by absorbing its
costs and managing the social problems which it creates. This
shifts the fundamental process of differentiation away from economic units (e.g. classes) and on to states. Therefore the modern
world-system differentiates into three types of state:

- core states that have a strong governmental structure integrated with a national culture, and that are developed,
  rich, and dominating within the system; late twentieth-
  century examples include the EU, Japan and the USA;
- peripheral areas, that have weak indigenous states and
  invaded cultures, and that are poor and therefore economically dependent on the core states; late twentieth-century
  examples include the 'newly industrializing countries' of
  the 'South' (i.e. in Asia, Africa and Latin America);
- semiperipheral areas, that include countries with moderately strong governmental structures, single-commodity or
  low-technology economies and that are therefore somewhat dependent on the core states; they may be earlier
  core states in decline or they may be emerging from the
  periphery; late twentieth-century examples include oil producers, former socialist states in Eastern Europe, and the
  'young dragon' societies of South-East Asia.

There is a division of labour between states in each of these
regions: 'tasks requiring higher levels of skill and greater capitalization are reserved for higher-ranking areas' (Wallerstein 1974:
350). However, the position of the semi-peripheral areas is of
special theoretical importance because their existence prevents
polarization and conflict between the core and the periphery.

Wallerstein is at pains to discuss the contingent connection
between international differentiation and the internal class structure. He concentrates mainly on the development of social classes,
in the Weberian sense of self-aware, class communities. One
example is the formation of a nationally restricted, bourgeois,

class consciousness in the sixteenth-century, European states in response to the emerging presence of a small, but noticeable working class. Importantly, these class formations articulate with world-system formations insofar as the social relations of production stabilize the world-system. The ability of core states to remain at the centre depends on their capacity to maintain capital accumulation in the face of working-class claims for redistribution.

Capitalism functions in relation to long-term cyclical rhythms, the central one of which is the regular, boom/bust pattern of expansion and contraction of the whole economy (Wallerstein 1990: 36). In a spectacular piece of anthropomorphism, he identifies one of the responses to this cyclical pattern:

> [T]he capitalist world-economy has seen the need to expand the geographic boundaries of the system as a whole, creating thereby new loci of production to participate in its axial division of labour. Over 400 years, these successive expansions have transformed the capitalist world-economy from a system located primarily in Europe to one that covers the entire globe.
>
> (1990: 36)

To be fair, Wallerstein does indicate that the consciousness of this need resides in the minds of the political, economic and military rulers of the world-system who deliberately employ multiple pressures to overcome resistance in areas being subjected to the process of 'incorporation'. One of the techniques they use is to 'sell' Western domination as the universalizing process of modernization which increases its palatability.

Although some have hailed Wallerstein's theory as a precursor of more genuine globalization theory (e.g. Giddens 1990: 68–70), his argument is fundamentally at odds with such formulations. For Wallerstein the mechanisms of geosystemic integration are exclusively economic – they are constituted as trading and exploitative relationships between relatively sovereign states and relatively independent cultures. By contrast, the genuine globalization theories reviewed in Chapter 3 propose a global unification of cultural orientations which 'turns on' and breaks down the barriers between national polities and local economies. More importantly, the existence of a world-system or systems does not itself imply global unification. Wallerstein's worlds are phenomenological not material. Several world-systems can co-exist on the planet. The world-system argument can only truly be a theory of globalization if it can give an account both of the incorporation of all states into a capitalist world-system and of the integration of polities and cultures by virtue of that expansion. The former is given in Wallerstein's recent statements on the cyclic nature of capitalist development, the possibility of political and cultural integration appears for the moment only to reside in his utopian formulation of world-socialism.

Although bearing a family resemblance to Wallerstein and Frank, Sklair's argument (1991) is an injunction to social scientists to pay more attention to transnational relationships that emerge under globalization and is therefore more explicitly a theory of it. The resemblance to Wallerstein lies in the argument that the global system of transnational practices is largely structured by capitalism. Transnational practices operate on three levels, analytically distinguished, the economic, the political and the cultural-ideological, each dominated by a major institution that heads the drive towards globalization. Respectively then, the main locus of transnational economic practices is the transnational corporation; of political practices, the transnational capitalist class; and of cultural-ideological practices, the culture of consumerism. Like the political scientists reviewed below, however, Sklair is equivocal about the balance of effectivity between transnational practices and nation-states. The nation-state is 'the spatial reference point' for them, the arena within which they intersect, but another, perhaps more significant reference point is: 'the global capitalist system, based on a variegated global capitalist class, which unquestionably dictates economic transnational practices, and is the most important single force in the struggle to dominate political and cultural-ideological transnational practices' (Sklair 1991: 7).

However, Sklair returns even the 'global' capitalist class to the internal workings of a national social system, albeit that of a hegemon: 'there is only one country, the United States, whose agents, organizations and classes are hegemonic in all three spheres' (1991: 7). In an argument reminiscent of Gilpin then (see below), it is hegemonic states that promote capitalism as the global system, Britain in the nineteenth century and the USA in the twentieth. Unlike Gilpin, however, Sklair attributes altruism to neither hegemon, holding them individually responsible for global inequalities constructed in their own interests.

TRANSNATIONAL CONNECTIONS

If globalization is a reality, it presents the discipline of political science with a considerable problem.[6] The chief focus of political science analysis, even more than of sociology, is the nation-state, and if globalization genuinely takes effect, the nation-state will be its chief victim. The main vehicle for the political analysis of global trends is the subdiscipline of International Relations (IR).[7] IR, with its focus on diplomacy, imperialism and war has always taken a global view of politics. The traditional IR view of these processes takes the form of what we might after Burton (1972: 28–32) call the 'snooker-ball model'.[8] Here each state is its own little globe and these balls are of various weights and colours. As they change through time – or move across the surface of the table – they interact with each other. Each ball has some 'autonomy' exerted upon it by the player (the agency of its own government) but as it moves its autonomy is limited by the positions and actions of the other balls (other states). In an extension of this model, the white ball might be a superpower.

International Relations has gone through many changes as it has adapted to transformations in the shape of international politics. However, the most recent shift, the one that coincides with the recent acceleration of globalization, is the most significant. It is beginning to encompass relations between economies and cultures that bypass primarily political agencies. In so doing it is reconstructing itself as a proto-theory of globalization. It must be described only as a proto-theory because all of its instances are dualistic. They retain a commitment to the continuing saliency of relations between states but accept that economic and cultural integrations develop alongside them.

Perhaps the first signal that International Relations needed to change was given by Burton (1972) himself. In what is essentially an undergraduate textbook Burton enjoins his readers to study not international relations but world society, a layering of inter-state relations with networks or systems relationships between individuals and collectivities that transcend or subvert state boundaries. If I can be forgiven a last extension of Burton's metaphors, this argument might lead us to conceive of the snooker table as being overlain by a cobweb of relatively fragile connections between the balls – when the balls move gently (diplomacy) they are guided by the strands, when they move violently (war) they disrupt them. The networks that Burton identifies are patterns based on such factors as trade, language, religious identification, ethnicity, ideology, strategic alliance, communications links, and legal and communications conventions. In a formulation that clearly prefigures true globalization theory he argues that we should replace a simplistic geographical notion of distance by one based on what he calls 'effective distance' (1972: 47). Here the more dense the systemic linkages between locations, effectively the closer they are. If we were to take Burton's argument to its extreme we would indeed have a genuine globalization theory – if the entire world is linked together by networks that are as dense as the ones which are available in local contexts then locality and geography will disappear altogether, the world will genuinely be one place and the nation-state will be redundant. However, for Burton, as for many other political scientists, this position remains much too radical because it denies the saliency of the state as a prime organizing principle of social life. He wants to insist that the world is dualistic, integrated at the substate level but still organized as segmented nation-states. Burton is not alone – dualism remains the bottom line for political science and International Relations versions of globalization. Bull (1977), for example, insists on the continuing saliency of what he calls the states system, a pattern of international relations in which there is a plurality of interacting sovereign states that accept a common set of rules and institutions. Bull identifies the clearest threat to the states system that he values so highly as the emergence of what he calls a 'new medievalism', a system of overlapping or segmented authority systems that undermines the sovereignty of states. He analyses this threat as four components that are generally consistent with the argument being offered in this book. They are:

- a tendency for states to amalgamate on a regional basis (e.g. the EU);
- the distintegration of states into constituent nationalities;
- the emergence of international terrorism;
- global technological unification.

However, Bull asserts that there is no evidence for the emergence of a world society that displaces the states system but his criterion for the emergence of a world society is too severe by most standards embracing: 'not merely a degree of interaction linking all parts of the human community to one another but a sense of common interest and common values, on the basis of which common rules and institutions may be built' (1977: 279). No self-respecting globalization theorist would subscribe to such a straw-person condition (see especially the review of Robertson's work in the subsequent Chapter 3). It does allow Bull happily to conclude, in the face of a great deal of evidence that he adduces to the contrary, that: 'the world political system of whose existence we have taken note in no way implies the demise of the states system'.[9]

Rosenau's analysis of emerging global interdependence is another example of what might be called a dualistic approach to the current transformation.[10] Rosenau's early work (1980) concentrates on what he calls 'transnationalization'. This is a process by which inter-governmental relations at an international level are supplemented by relations between non-governmental individuals and groups. Here Rosenau is a technological determinist much in the fashion of Kerr and his colleagues or Bell:

> Dynamic change, initiated by technological innovation and sustained by continuing advances in communications and transportation, has brought new associations and organizations into the political arena, and the efforts of these new entities to obtain external resources or otherwise interact with counterparts abroad have extended the range and intensified the dynamics of world affairs.
>
> (1980: 1–2)

So the proper study for a political science of world affairs is no longer simply 'international relations' but 'transnational relations' involving complex extra-societal relationships between governments, governmental and non-governmental international agencies, and non-governmental entities. Non-governmental inter-action rebounds onto states to produce an increasing level of interdependence between them and a disintegrative effect as it promotes intra-societal groups to the world stage. This involves: 'a transformation, even a breakdown of the nation-state system as it has existed throughout the last four centuries' (Rosenau 1980: 2). However, in what can only be regarded as a contradiction he insists that nation-states nevertheless remain the central actors. Some of their governments, he says, 'enjoy near total power to frame and execute policies' and all of them provide the main adaptive capacity for coping with change in the global system (1980: 3). We can only regard it as curious that they can manage to do this while simultaneously breaking down.

This dualism in Rosenau's analysis has not disappeared as it has matured. In his most recent work, in which globalization becomes much more explicit, he insists on what he calls the bifurcation of macro-global structures into 'the two worlds of world politics' (1990: 5). For this bifurcated system he now proposes to use the term 'postinternational politics' (1990: 6) implying that a simple snooker style pattern of international relations between states has now disappeared in the face of an unpredictable turbulence and chaos, that there is a very clear phase-shift under way.

Rosenau identifies five sources of this phase shift, beginning with his old friend, technology (1990: 12–13). They are:

- post-industrialization, forcing the development of micro-electronic technologies that reduce global distances by enabling the rapid movement of people, ideas and resources across the planet;[11]
- the emergence of planetary problems that are beyond the scope of states to resolve them;
- a decline in the ability of states to solve problems on a national basis;
- the emergence of new and more powerful subcollectivities within national societies;
- an increasing level of expertise, education and reflexive empowerment in the adult citizenry that makes them less susceptible to state authority.

Among these, the first, the 'technological dynamic' remains paramount:

> It is technology that has profoundly altered the scale on which human affairs take place, allowing people to do more things in less time and with wider repercussions than could have been imagined in earlier eras. It is tech-nology, in short, that has fostered an interdependence of local, national, and international communities that is far greater than any previously experienced.
>
> (Rosenau 1990: 17)

Rosenau can now make explicit the evolution of the bifurcated global structure (1990: 14). International relations emerged from the Second World War in 1945 dominated by two superpowers, the USA and the USSR, and their attached alliance blocs. This pattern was subjected to a decentralizing dynamic forced by changes in the planetary distributions of population and resources which led to the emergence of third-world states; and simultaneously to a centralizing dynamic forced by micro-electronic technological development which led to the development of governmental and non-governmental international organizations. By the 1960s this had introduced enough instability into the system to set the conditions for turbulence: individuals became more assertive and ungovernable; insoluble global problems emerged; subgroups and localisms were energized; and states began to appear incompetent. By the late 1980s the bifurcation had become manifest between: a state-centric world comprising relations between the USA, the USSR/Russia, the EC/EU, Japan, and the third world, and their links to international organizations and subgroups; and a 'multi-centric world' focused on relations between subgroups, international organizations, state bureaucracies and transnational actors (e.g. transnational corporations). The multi-centric world strives for autonomy from the state, the state-centric world for the security of political institutions. The contradiction between these principles pushes human society inexorably towards a manifest turbulence.

By contrast, a rather more conventional effort to preserve the saliency of the state is made by Gilpin (1987). Gilpin takes his lead from Marx and Wallerstein, linking globalization to the advance of capitalism. But it is a particular aspect of capitalism which attracts Gilpin's interest. The world will become globalized to the extent that the capitalist market, the process of commodification, expands and penetrates every corner of the planet: 'market competition and the responsiveness of actors to relative price changes propel society in the direction of increased specialization, greater efficiency, and ... the eventual economic unification of the globe' (1987: 65). The market, which is Gilpin's equivalent of Burton's systems or Rosenau's multi-centric world: 'is driven largely by its own internal dynamic' but, and here the schizoid tendency returns, the pace and direction of advance are 'profoundly affected by external factors' (Gilpin 1987: 65). It will come as no surprise to learn that among the most significant of these external factors is the domestic and international political framework. Again, we must recognize that if Gilpin wants to say that the state profoundly affects the direction and pace of marketization then very little effectivity can remain for its own internal logic.[12]

For Gilpin the capitalist market, and its globalizing effects, advance most effectively under conditions of geopolitical stability. Stability is a function of the extent to which the international political economy is dominated by a hegemonic superpower. And if the market is to succeed that hegemon must be liberal rather than authoritarian in its orientation. So: 'the existence of a hegemonic or dominant liberal power is a necessary (albeit not a sufficient) condition for the full development of a world market economy' (1987: 85). Where there is no hegemon to impose the conditions of freedom and perfection on the market the global economic system dissolves into a nationalistic and mercantilist competition in which states seek to monopolize demand and monopsonize supply.

There have been two main phases in which a liberal hegemony has prevailed, and consequently two main bursts of marketization/globalization. The first covered most of the nineteenth century when Britain was, in global terms, the dominant hegemonic power by virtue of its industrial head start, its colonial empire, and its naval military superiority. This was a period of relative international order and security, a period when international relations as a reflexive practice of diplomacy between states emerged. It was a period of treaties and alliances as well as an expanding global imperialism. The second was the briefer period between 1945 and 1970 when the USA was the global hegemon, drawing on its technological advantages, its mass production systems, and its military might. Through the Bretton Woods agreement it set up the International Monetary Fund (IMF) and the World Bank to stabilize exchange rates and curb international inflation; it set up the Marshall plan to underwrite the re-entry of the European economies into the world market; and it initiated GATT and the 'most favored nation' system to try to reduce international levels of tariff protection.

Gilpin now tries to turn conventional wisdom upon its head. That wisdom says that American hegemony declined with its inability to compete with Asian and European producers in world markets. Gilpin argues rather that America deliberately chose no longer to act as hegemon and in so doing opened up the international political economy to a triangular mercantilist dogfight. The international political economy is thus for him no longer truly globalized but rather consists of nationalistic attempts to succeed by beggaring neighbours through tax competition, migration prohibitions, investment subsidies, export subsidies, and import restraints. Often the actors in this process are regional groupings of states (e.g. Andean Pact, APEC, ASEAN, EU, NAFTA) but these act much as did the mercantilist states of the seventeenth and eighteenth centuries.

In a thesis full of contradiction Gilpin's solution to current economic problems is especially paradoxical. He calls for pluralist intervention to restore economic liberalism, that is for the triangle of dominating states to coordinate their policies in the direction of freedom of the market. Under the theory of hegemonic stability such a strategy cannot succeed. Indeed the slow progress achieved within such attempts as G7 economic summits and the Uruguay round of GATT negotiations would tend to confirm this proposition.

Arguably, these four political science accounts of globalization remain at the same level as world-system theory. They are prepared to admit the emergence of a world economic system but are unwilling to admit the possibility of the ultimate disintegration of nation-states and national cultures – indeed they often resort to a theoretical dualism in which contradictory causal effects are allowed to reside in separate parts of the theory. The global political economy is, for them, organized by the interactions of states. This is despite the fact that it is impossible to deny that multinational or transnational corporations are frequently more powerful than the states whose societies they operate in and that the extent to which cultural currents can transsect national borders is now greater than it has ever been. This narrowness of vision extends to an unwillingness to recognize the extent to which states are now surrendering sovereignty to international and supranational organizations as well as to more localized political units.

THE GLOBAL VILLAGE

In a world in which the minds of individuals are so resolutely focused on mass-mediated images it is surprising that so much social scientific attention should have been paid to global integration by means of economics and so little to culture or consciousness. This may well be because, as they stand, both sociology and political science are non-globalized and modern, as opposed to postmodern, disciplines. The main source of an alternative is the literary and communications theorist, McLuhan. Although much of McLuhan's work is unsatisfactory from the point of view of a positivistic or even an analytic social science, his ideas although formulated over thirty years ago, are so perceptive and insightful that they have insinuated themselves into many of the accounts that we now regard as ground-breaking. Indeed Giddens recent statements on globalization (see Chapter 3) clearly owe a substantial, though largely unacknowledged debt to McLuhan.

For McLuhan (1964) the determining principle of culture is the medium by which it is transmitted rather than its content. Media include any means of extending the senses and therefore include technologies of both transportation and communication. It follows that McLuhan's position anticipates the technological determinism of both Rosenau and Harvey (see Chapter 3). This allows a periodization of history into two principle epochs that roughly correspond with Durkheim's mechanical and organic solidarity. The first is what might be called the tribal epoch, which is based on the technologies of the spoken word and the wheel. In this oral culture human experience is necessarily instant, immediate and collective as well as subtle, sensitive and complete. The second is the industrial epoch based on technologies of the written word and of mechanization. In this literate culture, human experience is fragmented and privatized. Writing or reading a book is isolated and individualized, even lonely. Moreover, it emphasizes the sense of sight at the expense of sound, touch and smell, which leaves the viewer distant and unengaged. Print also constructs thought into connected lineal sequences that allow societies to rationalize and thereby to industrialize.

This transformation also had globalizing effects. The use of paper, wheels and roads allowed the first moves in the direction of what Giddens is later to call time-space distanciation (see Chapter 3). In their capacity to speed up communication, they started to connect distant localities, to reduce the consciousness of the tribe or village. They also allowed power centres to extend their control over geographic margins. Again anticipating Giddens and Harvey, McLuhan shows that this reorganization of space through time is accompanied by the development of two other important universalizing devices. First, the mechanical clock disrupted recursive and seasonal conceptions of time and replaced them by a durational conception where time is measured in precise divisions. Measured, universal time became an organizing principle for a modern world divorced from the immediacy of human experience. As McLuhan says, the division of labour begins with the division of time by the use of the mechanical clock (1964: 146). The second device is money (Giddens' 'symbolic tokens') which increases the speed and volume of relationships.

Current circumstances constitute a further epochal shift. The predominant industrial and individualizing media of print, the clock and money are being displaced by electronic media that restore the collective culture of tribalism but on an expansive global scale. Its key characteristic is speed. Because electronic communication is virtually instantaneous it drags events and locations together and renders them totally interdependent. Electricity establishes a global network of communication that is analogous to the human central nervous system. It enables us to apprehend and experience the world as a whole: 'with electricity we extend our central nervous system globally, instantly interrelating every human experience' (McLuhan 1964: 358). Lineal sequencing and thus rationality are dispatched by electronic speed-up and the synchronization of information – the world is experienced not simply globally but chaotically.

The accelerating effects of electronic communication and rapid transportation create a structural effect that McLuhan calls 'implosion' (1964: 185). By this he means that they, as it were, bring together in one place all the aspects of experience – one can simultaneously sense and touch events and objects that are great distances apart. The centre-margin structure of industrial civilization disappears in the face of synchrony, simultaneity and instantaneousness. In what has become an evocative and iconic formulation, McLuhan asserts that: 'This is the new world of the global village' (1964: 93).[13] Just as members of tribal society had been aware of their total interdependence with other members so members of the global village cannot avoid a consciousness of human society in its entirety. But global space is not at all similar to a tribal neighbourhood.

> Electric circuitry has overthrown the regime of 'time' and 'space' and pours upon us instantly and continuously the concerns of all other men. It has reconstituted dialogue on a global scale. Its message is Total Change, ending psychic, social, economic, and political parochialism. The old civic, state, and national groupings have become

unworkable. Nothing can be further from the spirit of the new technology than 'a place for everything and everything in its place.' You can't *go* home again.

(McLuhan and Fiore 1967: 16)

PREMONITIONS OF GLOBALIZATION

In the subsequent chapter we shall examine the burst of theorizing about globalization that accompanies its contemporary accelerated phase. These current social theorists have the benefit of the rear-vision mirror and also the prescient genius of Mashall McLuhan to stimulate their theorizing. However, it is clear from the above that, throughout the third quarter of the century, sociologists and political scientists have been at least dimly aware of this major social shift. The theoretical proposals that they offer can be summarized as follows:

1 The emergence of capitalism represents a major globalizing dynamic. Capitalism is such an effective form of production that it confers enormous power on those in control of it. This power can be used to subvert, control or bypass religious, political, military or other power resources.

2 Capitalism encompasses two major processes which tend to increase the level of societal inclusion. First it is driven by a logic of accumulation that depends on progressively increasing the scale of production. Second it is driven by a logic of commodification or marketization which drives it towards an increasing scale of consumption.

3 Capitalism also cloaks itself in the mantle of modernization. It offers the prospect not only of general and individual increases in the level of material welfare but of liberation from the constraints of tradition. This renders modernization unavoidable and capitalism compelling.

4 Modernization is more than an ideology however. Its differentiating trends release a series of activities from local and traditional contexts allowing them to be recombined nationally and transnationally.

5 A key emergent modern structure is the nation-state. It becomes the principle vehicle for the establishment of collective social goals and their attainment. Originally focused on security and on internal order and dispute

resolution, these goals have progressively become widened to include the management of both collective and individual material conditions, within the registers of the national economy and the welfare system.

6 The attainment of national goals obliged states to establish relations with other states and there emerged a system of international relations. The key processes of the nineteenth-century pattern of international relations were war, alliance, diplomacy, and colonialism. During the twentieth century these expanded to include trade, fiscal management, and cultural relations.

7 However, international relations are no longer the only links between societies. A stable system of international relations allowed the development of 'transnational practices', inter-societal linkages primarily focused on economic exchanges but also extending to tastes, fashions and ideas.

8 Electronic communications and rapid transportation are critical technologies for the development of these transnational practices. Their 'instant' character may have raised the possibility of a general cultural shift in a globalized direction.

We can now move on to examine the ways in which contemporary theorists of globalization have sought to integrate these proposals into general arguments about globalization.

3

Brave new worlds: recent theories

Now all the world's a sage
Marshall McLuhan and Quentin Fiore

Sociology is not immune to globo-babble. Just as politics, business, and the green social movement have been penetrated by references to the 'world', the 'planet' and the 'globe' so also have the social sciences. Coming hard on the heels of 'postmodernity' (Crook *et al.* 1992; Harvey 1989; Smart 1993), and although much less controversial, 'globalization' has become the buzzword of the 1990s in the analysis of social change. While the previous chapter is a catalogue of various social scientific attempts to map globalizing trends, this chapter focuses exclusively on the development and use of the concept itself.

As is noted in the Introduction, the concept of 'globalization' became current from about the mid-1980s onward. Its development as a specifically sociological concept owes by far the greatest debt to Roland Robertson of the University of Pittsburgh. However, it has also become a more widespread currency and in this chapter we survey not only Robertson's theory of globalization but also those of Giddens, Harvey, Beck and Lash and Urry.

THE WORLD AS 'ONE PLACE'

The key figure in the formalization and specification of the concept of globalization, then, is Robertson. His own biography might itself be seen as an instance of a link between what might be called transnationalization and global consciousness. He began his career in Britain where his initial studies sought to link the functionalist concept of modernization into an international context. At that time, like just about every other sociologist, he focused on the nation-state-society as the unit of analysis but he identified the nation-state as an actor in an international arena. By the 1970s Robertson had moved to the USA where initially he pursued studies in the sociology of religion. However his interpretation of religious developments was also essentially planetary in its orientation. Rejecting the prevailing commitment to secularization as the central social process, he became interested in developments in Islamic fundamentalism that indicated a link between religion and politics on a world scale. He was also interested in Weber's argument that Protestantism tended exactly to focus the consciousness on the material, as opposed to the spiritual world. He was thus able to return to his earlier interest in international society and his first general papers on globalization began to appear in the mid–1980s. By now the globe and its culture, rather than the nation-state, had become the primary concern. He had begun to untie the strait-jacket of the concept of national society which had left sociology out of touch with the big changes going on in the world and in which he had himself felt uncomfortable, from the beginning of his career:

> In an autobiographical sense my own perspective on this matter is undoubtedly to this day colored by the fact that one of my earliest, serious intellectual choices revolved around the question of whether I should study sociology or international relations as an undergraduate.
>
> (Robertson 1992: 4)

Robertson's first attempt to resolve this tension is contained in some work, partly undertaken with the political scientist, J.P. Nettl (1968), on the link between modernization and the international system of states. The key formulation is the argument that such an international system palpably exists, at least *in statu nascendi*. The notion of system is borrowed from Parsons and is an application of his well-known AGIL scheme (first developed in

Parsons and Smelser 1968). This argues that a complete system has structures or parts that function to resolve four system problems:

- adaptation to the environment (A);
- establishing practices for attaining goals (G);
- integrating exchanges between the parts of the system (I);
- latent provision for reproduction of the system over time (L).

In caricature then, in any social system there must be economic, political, community, and cultural activities. Nettl and Robertson (1968) are the first to admit that there is (or was in the 1960s) no completely formed international system. Rather, a process of system building was in train which was proceeding from the 'G subsystem' (international interaction between states), but met resistance in the form of unresolved cleavages in the cultural arena (L subsystem) that prevented full system development.

This is confirmed by what they call 'a cursory empirical examination' (Nettl and Robertson 1968: 150). Organizations of states seek to push out and 'systematize' the other three subsystems on an international scale. UNESCO and WHO, for example, engage the L subsystem, IPU and IATA the I subsystem, and the World Bank and ILO the A subsystem. At a higher level of abstraction, the international system of states was said to be actively engaged in:

- sharing power at an international, although normally continental, level to provide for collective security;
- establishing universal values and norms in, for example, the areas of political and social rights, the uses of nuclear power, and principles for the use of force;
- mitigating the distributional consequences of the international pattern of stratification by re-allocating economic resources; and
- co-ordinating exchanges between themselves in the areas of trade, migration, cultural performances, and so on.

But the development of the international system of states could only go as far as the cultural or L-subsystem would allow and here there were three significant cleavages within it preventing global systematization (Nettl and Robertson 1968: 152–62):

- the religious cleavage – here the focus is not on religious denominations per se but on general views of life and the world in terms of cognition and values; the cleavage is expressed in such distinctions as inner-directedness versus other-directedness, this-worldliness versus other-worldliness, theoreticism versus aestheticism, rationalism versus traditionalism, and linear conceptions of time versus cyclical conceptions;
- the legal-diplomatic cleavage between cultures for which international contact and 'the rule of law' are normal and regular on one hand and cultures that are internally oriented and absolutist on the other;
- the industrial cleavage, between cultures that emphasize norms consistent with industry (e.g. rationality, individualization, impersonal authority) and those that do not.

Global unification was prevented by religious and more specific cultural discontinuities which cleave the world in two dimensions characterized by the compass points. East (e.g. China) cleaves from West (e.g. USA) in religious and legal terms, while North (e.g. USSR) cleaves from South (e.g. Ethiopia) in diplomatic and industrial terms. However, Nettl and Robertson view the three as a hierarchy of levels with the highest degree of 'effectivity' or 'control' at the top. Religion, in the most general meaning of that term, is therefore the critical factor in globalization.

By the late 1980s it would appear from Robertson's recent work (1992) that the potential for a closing of these cleavages is greatly enhanced. He no longer speaks of an international system of states but of globalization at the cultural level. He begins by giving a two-part definition of the concept:

> Globalization as a concept refers both to the compression of the world and the intensification of consciousness of the world as a whole ... both concrete global interdependence and consciousness of the global whole in the twentieth century.
>
> (Robertson 1992: 8)

The first part of the definition, global compression, resembles the arguments of theories of dependency and of world-systems. It refers to an increasing level of interdependence between national systems by way of trade, military alliance and domination, and 'cultural imperialism'. Wallerstein (1974) tells us that the globe has been undergoing social compression since the beginning of the sixteenth century but Robertson argues that its history is in fact much longer. However, the more important component of the definition is the idea of an intensification of global consciousness which is a relatively new phenomenon. Robertson means by this an increasing probability that individual phenomenologies will be addressed to the entire world rather than to a local or national sector of it. This is true not only of such apparently cultural phenomena as the mass media and consumption preferences, in which it is relatively straightforward to conceive of a globalization of tastes, but also insofar as we culturally redefine or relativize all the issues we face in global terms. For example: we redefine military-political issues in terms of a 'world order'; or economic issues in terms of an 'international recession'; or marketing issues in terms of 'world' products (e.g. the 'world-car'); or religious issues in terms of ecumenism; or citizenship issues in terms of 'human rights'; or issues of pollution and purification in terms of 'saving the planet'.

This rise in global consciousness, along with higher levels of material interdependence, increases the probability that the world will be reproduced as a single system. Thus Robertson claims that the world is becoming more and more united, although he is careful not to say that it is becoming more and more integrated. While it is a single system, it is riven by conflict and there is by no means universal agreement on what shape the single system should take in the future.

In its peculiar, twentieth-century manifestation of a holistic consciousness, globalization involves the relativization of individual and national reference points to general and supranational ones. It therefore involves the establishment of cultural, social and phenomenological linkages between four elements (Robertson 1992: 25–31):

1 the individual self;
2 the national society;
3 the international system of societies; and
4 humanity in general.

Taken together, these constitute the 'global field', the range of objects we need to consider in analysing globalization. Under globalization the following phenomenological linkages and relativizations start to be made between these elements:

- The individual self (1) is defined as a citizen of a national society (2), by comparison with developments in other societies (3), and as an instance of humanity (4).
- A national society (2) stands in a problematical relationship to its citizens (1) in terms of freedom and control, views itself to be a member of a community of nations (3), and must provide citizenship rights that are referenced against general human rights (4).
- The international system (3) depends on the surrender of sovereignty by national societies (2), sets standards for individual behaviour (1), and provides 'reality checks' on human aspirations (4).
- Humanity (4) is defined in terms of individual rights (1) that are expressed in the citizenship provisions of national societies (2) which are legitimated and enforced through the international system of societies (3).

These interactions produce processual developments at each of the four reference points, namely: individualization, the global redefinition of each person as a complete whole rather than as a subordinate part of any localized collectivity; internationalization, the multiplication of inter-state interdependencies and arrangements; societalization, the establishment of the 'modern' nation-state as the only possible form of society; and humanization, the global establishment of the view that humanity cannot be differentiated by race, class or gender in terms of its possibilities and rights (Robertson 1992: 282–6). Taken together these constitute the social processes of globalization. These developments occur independently of the internal dynamics of individual societies. Indeed, globalization has its own 'inexorable' logic which will inevitably affect these internal dynamics.

Robertson insists that the process of globalization is not new, that it predates modernity and the rise of capitalism. However modernization tends to accelerate globalization and the process has moved to the level of consciousness during the contemporary period. Moreover, European civilization is the central focus for and origin of the development. He maps the path of globalization as a series of five phases (1992: 58–60):

I *The germinal phase* (Europe, 1400–1750)
- dissolution of Christendom and emergence of state communities

- Catholic (i.e. universal) churches
- development of generalizations about humanity and the individual
- first maps of the planet
- sun-centred universe
- universal calendar in the West
- global exploration
- colonialism

II *The incipient phase* (Europe, 1750–1875)
- nation-state
- formal diplomacy between states
- citizenship and passports
- international exhibitions and communications agreements
- international legal conventions
- first non-European nations
- first ideas of internationalism and universalism.

III *The take-off phase* (1875–1925)
- conceptualization of the world in terms of the four globalizing reference points – the nation-state, the individual, a single international society, and a single (masculine) humanity
- international communications, sporting and cultural links
- global calendar
- first ever world war, so defined
- mass international migrations and restrictions thereon
- more non-Europeans in the international club of nation-states.

IV *The struggle-for-hegemony phase* (1925–69)
- League of Nations and UN
- Second World War; Cold War
- conceptions of war crimes and crimes against humanity
- the universal nuclear threat of the atomic bomb
- emergence of the Third (part of the) World.

V *The uncertainty phase* (1969–92)
- exploration of space;
- post-materialist values and rights discourses;
- world communities based on sexual preference, gender, ethnicity and race;

- international relations more complex and fluid;
- global environmental problems recognized;
- global mass media via space technology (satellite television, etc.).

The 1990s are uncertain he argues because we (the inhabitants
of the planet) have little confidence in the direction in which we
are heading and only a little more in the direction of the planetary
environment.

These developments occur independently of the internal
dynamics of individual societies. Indeed, globalization has its own
logic which will inevitably affect these internal dynamics. This
logic, Robertson insists, has its roots in the emergence of the
culturally homogeneous nation-state in the middle of the eighteenth century: 'the diffusion of the *idea* of the national society
as a form of institutionalized societalism ... was central to the
accelerated globalization which began just over a hundred years
ago' (1992: 58, original italics). Robertson does not make explicit
this logic but the steps might be: nation-states are bounded social
systems; they will compete for resources and markets and they
will not necessarily be materially self-sufficient; they will therefore
engage in economic, military, political (diplomatic) and cultural
exchanges across the boundaries that are both co-operative and
conflictual; differential outcomes and therefore cross-national
mimesis will ensue; states will seek to systematize international
relations in order to secure the conditions of their own existence.

The particular outcome that separates globalization in the
contemporary period from its earlier manifestations is its reflexivity: 'the world "moved" from being merely "in itself" to the
problem or possibility of being "for itself"' (1992: 55). Injunc-
tions from the diverse viewpoints of both business consultants and
environmentalists to 'think globally' mean that the inhabitants of
the planet set out to make it, in the terms Robertson borrows
from Giddens, to structurate it as a whole, to apprehend it as
'one place' (Robertson and Garrett 1991: ix). On this argument,
people conceptualize the world as a whole, so they reproduce it
as a single unit and in turn increase the probability that this is
the way in which it will be conceived.

Robertson makes numerous careful reservations about his
argument. He claims that globalization, for example, is neither
necessarily a good nor a bad thing – its moral character will be
accomplished by the inhabitants of the planet. He is also not

saying that the world is, as a consequence of globalization, a more integrated or harmonious place but merely that it is a more unified or systematic place. He means by this that while events in any part of the world will increasingly have consequences for, or be referenced against events in other distant parts, this relativization may not always be positive. Indeed, the world as a system may well be riven by conflicts that are far more intractable than the previous disputes between nations. However he is saying the following: first that world is experiencing accelerated globalization to such an extent that it can be regarded as an accomplishment; second, that we need new concepts to analyse this process; third, that the process is fundamentally cultural and reflexive in character; and fourth that globalization follows the path of its own inexorable logic.

Not all theorists accept Robertson's view that the cultural cleavages that might prevent globalization have now been closed. Kavolis (1988), for example, would argue that such a view represents a peculiarly Western version of culture in which religion is conceived to be an increasingly subordinate subset of it. Rather, under Islam, for example, culture is enclosed by and is subordinate to religion. To the extent, then, that religion determines the moral-cultural sphere and to the extent that religions offer differential moral codes we can identify separated civilizational structures that constrain individual action. World culture is, for Kavolis, divided into at least seven such incommensurable civilizational systems: Christian, Chinese (Confucian-Taoist-Buddhist), Islamic, Hindu, Japanese (Shinto-Buddhist-Confucian), Latin American syncretist, and non-Islamic African (Kavolis 1988: 210–12). Robertson's globalization theory, for him, represents an argument for desacralization in favour of a humanistic ecumenism – Kavolis objects particularly to Robertson's use of the term 'global humanity'. For his part Robertson (1992: 129–37) claims that he does not deny the particularities of individual religions but insists on their relativization. Globalization brings their differences into sharp contrast and forces them to respond to the claims of other religions.

REFLEXIVITY AND TIME-SPACE DISTANCIATION

If it is the case that globalization is a predominant pattern in contemporary social change then it should not come as a surprise that several sociologists should hit on the concept at the same time. Robertson's chief rival for the mantle of parent of the concept is Anthony Giddens.[1]

Giddens first addresses the issue of the emergence of a global system in a general critique of Marxist theory in which he challenges the view that the development of the capitalist system alone determines the modern history of human societies arguing that it is also determined by the development of nation-states and their capacity to wage war on one another (1981; 1985). The nation-state has become the universal political unit so that the world is a network of national societies represented by their states in a global system of international relations. For Giddens, as for Robertson, the ascendency of the nation-state is coterminous with the development of that system of international relations. Each is impossible without the other.

Giddens explains the universalization of the nation-state in three sets of terms (1985: 255–7). First, those 'imagined communities', the European nation-states of the nineteenth century (especially Britain, France, Germany, and Italy) were able successfully to marry industrial production to military action. This industrialization of warfare made them particularly successful in military encounters with tribal societies, which they colonized, and with absolutist empires, which they dismembered. Second, their rational-bureaucratic characteristics made them particularly effective in harnessing resources in the service of national development and in managing relations with other nation-states through diplomatic networks and transnational political agencies. Third, a set of historical contingencies, the most important of which were the long peace of the nineteenth century, allowed the European states to concentrate economic resources on industrialization and colonization. A second contingency, the destabilization of international relations by the World Wars of the twentieth century forced the reflexive establishment of an international military order incorporating both superpower hegemony and international peacekeeping systems. However, the burgeoning development of international organizations during the twentieth century does not, Giddens insists, imply a loss of sovereignty for the nation-state but rather the securitization and institutionalization of that sovereignty. The reflexive system of international relations affirms the territorial and ethnic integrity of individual nation-states. Indeed, it provides a secure environment in which new states, however small and weak, can emerge and to some extent prosper.

In his later work Giddens links the process of globalization to the development of modern societies. A modern society, that is a post-feudal European society or any of its more recent copies, has four institutional characteristics or 'organisational clusters' (1990: 55–63; 1991: 15). The first two of these are broadly economic in character. Modernity involves, first, a capitalist system of commodity production that involves a social relationship between the owners of private capital and non-owners who sell their labour for wages. Enterprises compete in markets for capital, labour, raw materials and components, and products. Second, modernity implies industrialism, the multiplication of human effort by the application of inanimate sources of power channelled through machines. The scale of this technology implies a collective process of production in which the activities of a number of individuals are co-ordinated in the pursuit of an accumulation of material resources.

As we have seen, however, Giddens' main message is that a modern society is not defined entirely by its economic base but by the fact that it is a nation-state. A specific feature of the nineteenth-century European nation-state was its administrative competence, its capacity to establish co-ordinated control over a population within a defined territory. The main social technology that allowed the state to achieve this was the development of Foucauldian surveillance techniques. There are two varieties of surveillance: the ability to collect abstracted and coded sets of information about individuals; and the establishment of hierarchical systems of supervision that allow populations to be watched. A second specific feature of the modern nation-state is the centralization of control of the means of violence within an industrialized military order.

Thus the capitalist nation-state is the modern society *par excellence* because it embodies the extreme development of these four characteristics. This development is driven by certain dynamic processes. In a McLuhanist formulation, the primary process is the distanciation or separation of time from space (Giddens 1990: 17–21; 1991: 16–17). In premodern contexts both time and space were fundamentally linked to a person's immediate location. The temporal rhythms of everyday life were determined by local diurnal and seasonal cycles. Equally space was confined to what one immediately could perceive and was measured in relation to one's home location, even if one travelled. In the eighteenth century the invention and diffusion of the mechanical clock had the effect of universalizing time, prising it away from particular localities and allowing its social reorganization into a global system of zones. Equally space, as expressed in global maps, became a universal social dimension whose reality is independent of any individual social location. The liberation of time and space is an entirely modernizing development because it allows the stable organization of human activity across vast temporal and spatial distances – it is a prerequisite for globalization.

Time-space distanciation is also a prerequisite for the modernizing process that Giddens calls disembedding: 'the lifting out' of social relations from local contexts of interaction and their restructuring across time and space' (1990: 21). He identifies two types of disembedding mechanism: symbolic tokens (c.f. McLuhan) and expert systems. The former are such universal media of exchange as money, which is the only such medium to which Giddens devotes much analysis. Money can transfer value from context to context and can thus make social relations possible across great expanses of time and space. Expert systems consist of repositories of technical knowledge that can be deployed across a wide range of actual contexts. An expert system gives guarantees about what to expect across all of these contexts. Each of these disembedding mechanisms implies an attitude of trust, that is, that people have confidence in the value of money and in the accuracy of expertise that is produced by non-present others. Modernity therefore involves both high trust and high risk.

The fact that moderns trust their societies and their lives to be guided by impersonal flows of money and expertise does not mean that they allow such developments to proceed in an unmonitored way. Aware of risk, they constantly watch, seek information about, and consider the value of money and the validity of expertise. Modern society is therefore specifically reflexive in character. Social activity is constantly informed by flows of information and analysis which subject it to continuous revision and thereby constitute and reproduce it. 'Knowing what to do' in modern society, even in such resolutely traditional contexts as kinship or childrearing, almost always involves acquiring knowledge about how to do it from books, or television programmes, or expert consultations, rather than relying on habit, mimesis or authoritative direction from elders. The particular difficulty faced by moderns is that this knowledge itself is constantly changing so that living in a modern society appears to be uncontrolled, like being aboard a careering juggernaut as Giddens has it. Giddens goes so far as to argue that sociology has a pivotal position in this reflexion on social relations and that, as a consequence: 'Modernity is itself deeply and intrinsically sociological' (1991: 43, italics deleted). Practitioners of the discipline might have more confidence in its future if this statement was only half-true. Certainly if we were to insert the name of that 'dismal' social science, economics, into the quotation we would have little difficulty in agreeing with it.

The reader might well now be wondering whether this book might be an introduction to 'modernization' rather than to 'globalization'. The reason for this extensive treatment of Giddens' theory of modernization is that, contra Robertson, he views globalization as its direct consequence. Each of the three main dynamics of modernization implies universalizing tendencies which render social relations ever more inclusive. They make possible global networks of relationships, (e.g. the system of international relations or the modern world-system of capitalism), but they are also, for Giddens, more fundamental in extending the temporal and spatial distance of social relationships. Time-space distanciation, disembedding, and reflexivity mean that complex relationships develop between local activities and interaction across distances. Security of employment for an Australian sheep shearer, for example, might be affected by trends in Japanese fashions, the 'Uruguay' round of GATT negotiations, the cost of synthetic fibres which is in turn be determined by the price of oil which might in turn be determined by American military intervention in the Persian Gulf, and the extent to which the Australian Government accepts prevailing global ideologies of marketization and privatization.

> Globalisation can thus be defined as the intensification of worldwide social relations which link distant localities in such a way that local happenings are shaped by events occurring many miles away and vice versa. This is a dialectical process because such local happenings may move in an obverse direction from the very distanciated relations that shape them. Local transformation is as much a part of globalisation as the lateral extension of social connections across time and space.
>
> (Giddens 1990: 64, italics deleted)

Giddens' insistence that local transformations are part of the globalization process helps to explain why local nationalisms, such as those emerging in the 1980s and 1990s in Catalonia, or Bosnia-Hercegovina, or Tamil Elam (in Sri Lanka), are not counter-globalization developments. They are precisely the consequence of the global spread of institutions of national self-determination, democratization, and administrative rationalization.

Giddens can now proceed to discuss the institutional directions in which globalization takes the world in terms of his four dimensions of modernity (capitalism, surveillance, military order and industrialism) (1990: 70–8). First the world economy is increasingly constituted as a capitalist world-system, in Wallerstein's terms. The world economy is dominated by trans-national corporations that operate independently of political arrangements and indeed can achieve economic domination over them. These corporations set up global linkages and systems of exchange so that the globe is increasingly constituted as a single market for commodities, labour and capital. It is no longer necessary to explain, as both Giddens and Wallerstein had to, the persistence of state socialist economies. They have collapsed in Russia and Eastern Europe and the one in China is being transformed in a capitalist direction.

The surveillance process is also being extended in global directions in a system of nation-states. We have already considered the point that the sovereignty of a state is enhanced by mutual and reflexive recognition of sovereignty. International organizations fix sovereignty and allow the incorporation of former colonies into the nation-state system. Beyond this argument from Giddens, it might be suggested that cooperation between states in international organizations, the pooling of information and expertise, increases the capacity of a state to oversee its own population and, indeed, to intefere in the oversight of the populations of other states.

The key to the development of a world military order is the alliance system. Giddens points to a bipolar, superpower alliance system of truly global scope, although this has now been superseded by the 'new world order', a monocentric alliance system built around the military dominance of the USA and which now merges with UN peacekeeping operations. War itself has also been globalized through the two 'World Wars' and the global 'Cold War' (the stand-off of mutually assured destruction

(MAD) between the two superpowers) that dominated military thinking for most of the second half of the twentieth century. It may currently be the case that world war has become so globalized as to have become impossible, so that only local and peripheral conflicts, referenced against global alliances, have much chance of occurring.

The globalization of industrialism involves the incorporation of local industries into an international division of labour in which there is an increasing level of trade in raw materials, components and commodities between previously separate and complete industrial economies. This development includes the diffusion of machine and other industrial technologies and collective but rationalized production systems. This industrialization of the world has eroded Western economic dominance but it has had significant consequences in two other arenas. First, industrialism is reflexively recognized as having a harmful effect on the ecology of the planet as a whole. Second, industrialization has long since gone beyond the production of commodities to cover services and information. The industrialization of culture via what have become known as the mass media has carried with it the globalization of culture, especially its consumption-centred components. Curiously, while cultural globalization is Giddens' last thought on the topic and receives scant attention he nevertheless feels able to describe it as: 'a fundamental aspect of globalisation, which lies behind each of the various institutional dimensions that have been mentioned' (1990: 77). If the globalization of culture is the axial determinant of the process it might deserve a more prominent treatment.

Last minute thoughts not withstanding, globalization is then for Giddens a multi-causal and multi-stranded process which is full of contingency and uncertainty. Globalization appears to be inexorable but because the imperatives that propel the world forward on the juggernaut of modernization are contained within four, relatively insulated arenas, particular outcomes are unpredictable. Globalization: 'is a process of uneven development that fragments as it coordinates' (Giddens 1990: 175).

Lash and Urry's application of concepts of time-space distanciation and reflexivity (1994), while influenced by Giddens, arrives at a distinctly different conclusion about the nation-state. Their analysis takes off from an earlier book about the decomposition of what they call 'organized capitalism' (1987). Under organized (twentieth century) capitalism flows of finance, commodities, means of production and labour are tightly arranged in time and space by large business corporations and states. Disorganized capitalism involves an expansion of these flows in the international arena and an increase in their velocity (see Chapter 4). Speed and the reduction of time invade culture, it becomes postmodern, focused on instant consumption and flexibility in the application of labour. However, objects are not the only items that become highly mobile in a postmodern world, individual persons or subjects also become mobile by means of migration, instrumental travel and tourism. And as objects become more mobile they progressively dematerialize and are produced as symbols ('signs').

Two sorts of sign are possible: cognitive signs, symbols that represent information; and aesthetic signs, symbols that represent consumption. Their proliferation, in turn, promotes two kinds of reflexivity. First it promotes a pattern of what they call 'reflexive accumulation', the individualized self-monitoring of production and of expertise and an accompanying increasing and widespread tendency to question authority and expertise. Second, it promotes an aesthetic or expressive reflexivity in which individuals constantly reference self-presentation in relation to a normatized set of possible meanings given in the increasing flow of symbols – people monitor their own images and deliberately alter them.

The contemporary global order, Lash and Urry argue, is therefore: 'a structure of flows, a de-centred set of economies of signs in space'. Insofar as these flows of symbols are undermining nation-state societies we can identify a process of globalization. This involves (1994: 280–1):

- the development of transnational practices (see Chapter 2 on Rosenau);
- the development of localized sites, 'global cities' that originate transnational practices (see King 1990b);
- a decreasing effectivity of state policy instruments (see Chapter 5);
- an increasing number of inter-state connections (see Chapter 5);
- the embryonic development of global bureaucracies (see Chapter 5);
- the emergence of new socio-spatial political entities (see Chapter 5 and Chapter 6 on ethnic nationalism);
- an overall decline in the sovereignty of the state.[2]

POSTMODERNITY AND TIME-SPACE COMPRESSION

Giddens is notable within the current upsurge of interest in general social change for his insistence that current transformations constitute a continuation of rather than a break with modernity. While such postmodernists as Lyotard (1984) would point to current uncertainties as the consequence of the collapse of foundationalist meta-narratives that previously attempted to provide comprehensive answers to questions of human existence, Giddens argues that there is nothing new in this. Modernity has always created uncertainty and as the juggernaut gathers speed the incapacity of knowledge systems to tell what to do becomes chronic. Giddens characterizes the contemporary period as a high or radicalized modernity in which concerted action on a global scale is increasingly probable, although linked to processes of dispersal and localization. Postmodernity is for him a utopian condition in which human beings have resolved their problems within each of the four organizational clusters of modernity. A postmodern society would incorporate: a post-scarcity economy; multilevel political participation, especially at the local level; the humanization of technology; and global demilitarization (Giddens 1990: 164). The inertial drag of modernity not withstanding, Crook *et al.* (1992) argue, in opposition to Giddens, that many aspects of these clusters are in fact emerging in a process of postmodernization, although not as the consequence of future-oriented, intentional utopian thought but of the dialectics of modernity itself.

The issue of a connection between postmodernization and globalization is the source of much theoretical speculation, most notably by Smart (1993: 127–53) drawing on Appadurai (1990). However the key figure in establishing the link is the geographer, David Harvey (1989). The link is established through concepts of time and space similar to those used by Giddens. Like Giddens, Harvey begins with an analysis of premodern conceptions of space and time (1989: 239–59), although the issue of space is here held to be primary. In the feudal context space was conceived within the terms of a relatively autonomous community that involved a fused pattern of economic, political and religious rights and obligations. Equally, temporal organization was determined by community rhythms. Space outside the community was only dimly perceived, time even more so. These localized conceptions of space and time were only reconstructed during the renaissance as European voyages of discovery established the limits of space, the planet was discontinuous with the cosmos and could therefore be mapped and objectivated and, in art, perspectivized. The mechanical watch equally reconstituted time as a linear and universal process.

Here, Harvey's analysis departs from Giddens. Giddens has time differentiating from space. More convincingly, Harvey argues that the objectification and universalization of concepts of space and time allowed time to annihilate space. He calls this process time-space compression, a development in which time can be reorganized in such a way as to reduce the constraints of space, and vice versa. Time-space compression involves a shortening of time and a 'shrinking' of space – progressively, the time taken to do things reduces and this in turn reduces the experiential distance between different points in space. We might argue that if people in Tokyo can experience the same thing at the same time as others in Helsinki, say a business transaction or a media event, then they in effect live in the same place, space has been annihilated by time compression. Harvey (1989: 241) illustrates the process in a diagram which shows four maps of the world over time, each smaller than the previous with size determined by the speed of transportation. The world of the 1960s is about one-fiftieth the size of the world of the sixteenth century precisely because jet aircraft can travel at about fifty times the speed of a sailing ship.

The process of time-space compression is not gradual and continuous but occurs in short and intense bursts during which the world changes rapidly and uncertainty increases. In a Marxisant analysis, Harvey attributes these bursts to crises of overaccumulation in the capitalist system. One such burst occurred in the second half of the nineteenth century and is associated with the cultural movement known as modernism (Harvey 1989: 260–283). The crisis occurred as a collapse of credit in 1847–8 due to overspeculation in railroad construction (i.e. an attempt to control space) and was resolved by the establishment of unified European capital and credit markets organized by a pan-European class of financial capitalists. Time was compressed as capital flowed more rapidly through this reorganized system and this provided the springboard for the further conquest of space by investment in railroads, canals, shipping, pipelines, and telegraphy. Towards the turn of the century space shrunk further with inventions in ground transport (the bicycle and automobile), aviation (the balloon, the aircraft), and communication (wireless telegraphy, radio, TV, mass printing, photography, cinema).

Europe established colonial hegemony over the planetary surface. Henry Ford reorganized the space of production into an assembly-line, thus reducing the time (and cost) of production, thereby allowing a further reorganization of space in mass production terms. Industrialized mass production and rapid transportation fuelled the first global war of 1914–18 and this in turn allowed a reorganization of territorial space under the Versailles agreements. By 1920 global systems of finance capital and of international relations had been established and mass production had become the predominant pattern of industrial organization.

In about 1970, argues Harvey (1989: 159–72), a further burst of time-space compression began. It began with an over-accumulation crisis in the system of mass production. Fordist mass production had become so successful and efficient that workers began to be laid off, thus effectively reducing demand for products, at the same time as output was expanding rapidly. Consumer markets were saturated to such an extent that governments were unable to correct the imbalances and were also unable to meet the commitments entailed in their welfare programmes. Their only response was to print money and thereby to set in train a wave of uncontrollable inflation. The crisis shook the system to such an extent that it actually began to tackle the rigidities entailed in the mass production process – the corporatist compromises between management and workers and the management of consumer markets to accept standardized products. A regime of 'flexible accumulation' emerged in which flexibly contracted workers use their multiple skills and computerized machinery to dovetail products to rapidly shifting tastes. As in the nineteenth century, some of the earliest and most profound effects were felt in the structures of financial markets. They have experienced the typical globalizing trends of long-range international links on one hand and decentralization and dispersal on the other. There is no longer a finance capitalist class that runs the system – it is chaotic, continuous, fluid and of enormous scope. It has also become much more powerful, subordinating the actions of both national governments and transnational corporations to market constraints. National fiscal policy, for example, is subjected to constant reflexive checks via floating currency exchange rates. The outcome is truly globalizing:

> The formation of a global stock market, of global commodity (even debt) futures markets, of currency and

interest rate swaps, together with an accelerated geographical mobility of funds, meant, for the first time, the
formation of a single world market for money and credit
supply.

The structure of this global financial system is now
so complicated that it surpasses most people's understanding. The boundaries between distinctive functions
like banking, brokerage, financial services, housing
finance, consumer credit, and the like have become
increasingly porous at the same time as new markets in
commodity, stock, currency, or debt futures, have sprung
up, discounting future into present time in baffling ways.
Computerization and electronic communications have
pressed home the significance of instantaneous international co-ordination of financial flows.

(Harvey 1989: 161)

Flexible accumulation itself represents a particular form of time
compression. It was principally directed at reductions in turnover
time, the period between the acquisition of components and the
delivery of products, by the development of outsourcing, 'just-in-
time' inventory systems, and small batch production. In its turn
consumption patterns have experienced a similar temporal compression. If taste is the only determinant of utility then that utility
is ephemeral and subject to whim. Product demand is determined
by fashion and unfashionable products are disposable. The most
instant and disposable of products are mass-mediated images that
are lost the moment that they are consumed. Insofar as images
have no past and no future, human experience becomes compressed into an overwhelming present.

The above argument would have no direct relevance to the
issue of globalization was it not for Harvey's argument that
the compression of time annihilates space (1989: 293–5). The last
two decades represent: 'another fierce round in that annihilation
of space through time that has always lain at the center of capitalism's dynamic' (1989: 293). Here Harvey gives us another version
of McLuhan's global village. He writes of the way in which satellite technologies have made the cost of communication invariant
with respect to distance, the reduction in international freight
rates, the global rush of images via satellite television which
provides a universal experience, and the way in which mass tourism can make that experience direct. Spatial barriers have

collapsed so that the world is now a single field within which capitalism can operate and capital flows become more and more sensitive to the relative advantages of particular spatial locations. Paradoxically, as consumption becomes universalized through globally available brands, production can become localized according to cost advantages – so, for example, Levi jeans are available globally but are produced in the low-labour-cost environment of the Philippines, and many of the 'Big Macs' sold in Europe contain Australian shredded lettuce, airfreighted overnight.

Harvey's version of the importance of time and space is preferable to that of Giddens because Giddens' term 'distanciation' leaves the impression that time and space are becoming stretched. This is not, of course, the meaning that he intends, which is rather that social relationships are becoming stretched across great distances. Even this is misleading however – new communications technologies are ensuring that transglobal social relationships, say between kin or colleagues, are becoming more intense and robust rather than stretched and attenuated. Harvey's notion of compression of social relationships so that spatial distance becomes unimportant fits the proposal of a globalizing trend far more closely. What is unsatisfactory in Harvey is his determination to cling to historical, or in his own terms, historical-geographical materialism as an explanatory logic. The link between flexible accumulation and globalization is tenuous at best, even if it could be confirmed that flexible accumulation has been successfully institutionalized. Harvey leaps from the incipient practices of JIT inventories and contractualization to global capital flows and mass mediated images. It is surely possible that the advantages which instant electronic communication offers to the latter developments would have been decisive even if there had been no accumulation crisis.

RISK AND ECOLOGICAL APPROPRIATION

We have seen that Giddens views the reorganization of risk as an important feature of the dynamics of modernity. Because we trust both monetary tokens and non-present experts we run the fiduciary risk of a collapse in value which is beyond our individual or local control. The German sociologist, Ulrich Beck (1992)[3] places risk at the centre of his analysis of contemporary social change.

From the viewpoint of the most economically advanced

sectors of the world, Beck argues, we are already living in a post-scarcity society. Contemporary society has moved out of the phase in which it was predominantly oriented to technological applications that would maximize the flow of material resources and in which the main practices of the state were to effect a fair and just distribution of these material returns through a welfare system. In that modernization phase people had been prepared to accept medical and ecological side-effects in return for an increase in material welfare. But now things have changed:

> In the welfare states of the West a double process is taking place now. On the one hand, the struggle for one's 'daily bread' has lost its urgency as a cardinal problem overshadowing everything else, compared to material subsistence in the first half of this century, and to a Third World menaced by hunger. For many people problems of 'overweight' take the place of hunger. . . . Parallel to that, the knowledge is spreading that the sources of wealth are 'polluted' by growing 'hazardous side effects'.
> (Beck 1992: 20)

These side-effects constitute risks and the distribution of these risks is becoming the central feature of affluent societies. An important defining feature of risk is its social reflexivity. It is not the hazards themselves that are new and special but the way in which they are socially constituted: 'Risk may be defined as a systematic way of dealing with hazards and insecurities induced and introduced by modernization itself' (1992: 21, italics deleted). The risks of which we are becoming increasingly conscious, both scientifically and politically, include threats from radioactivity, toxins and pollutants that cause long-term, irreversible and invisible damage to organisms.

These risks, argues Beck, are qualitatively different from the hazards and dangers experienced in previous periods of history. First, the current risks are the direct consequence of industrialization and are implicit and unavoidable within it, they are not the risks of intentional adventure. Second, the risks we currently experience in the forms of trace toxins or radioactivity are no longer perceptible to the senses. Third, they do not derive from undersupply of technology or wealth but from overproduction. Indeed as industrialization intensifies on a global scale, the risks multiply. Fourth, the contemporary experience of risk is scientifically and politically reflexive. Society is intentionally recast as an attempt to reduce risk but cannot deal with: 'the threatening force of modernization and its globalization of doubt' (Beck 1992: 21). Fifth contemporary risks are not tied to their local origins but: 'By their nature they endanger all forms of life on this planet' (1992: 22, italics deleted). Such ecological and 'high-tech' risks as nuclear accidents and acid rain admit of no boundary in time or space – once present they are continuous and general. Sixth, the globalization of high-risk industries means that the scientific calculation of risk and of its consequences has become impossible.

Risk has a double saliency in relation to globalization. As is clear from the above, Beck reckons modernization to be the primary globalizing force. Global risks are the product of global industrialization. But because risk is itself inherently globalizing, the advent of risk society accelerates the globalization process. It is in terms of this effect that Beck makes his contribution to the conceptualization of globalization. Risk globalizes because it universalizes and equalizes. It affects every member of society regardless of location and class position. Moreover it respects no border:

> Food chains connect practically everyone on earth to everyone else. They dip under borders. The acid content of the air is not only nibbling at sculptures and artistic treasures, it also long ago brought about the disintegration of modern customs barriers. Even in Canada the lakes have become acidified, and forests are dying even in the northern reaches of Scandinavia.
>
> (Beck 1992: 36)

The reflexive character of risk, combined with its lack of boundedness in space, forces consciousness in the direction of globalization. The only possible solutions to risk are supranational solutions: strategic arms reduction talks, earth summits, international agreements on emission reduction or the use of CFCs, nuclear weapons proliferation agreements.

Risk distribution in the globalized system follows a pattern that Beck calls the 'boomerang curve'. Here, the hazardous consequences of risk return to their sources and adversely affect those who produce them. In the previous period of modernization risk had been a latent side effect from which the rich and powerful could insulate themselves but now risk returns to haunt the very centres of production. This is especially apparent in industrialized agriculture where the use of artificial irrigation, fertilizers and pesticides can actually destroy land and increase the immunity levels of pests. The universalizing-localizing paradox of globalization theory is present here too then: 'under the roof of modernization risks, perpetrator and victim sooner or later become identical' (Beck 1992: 38). The paramount risk in this syndrome is the (albeit receding) risk of a global nuclear war in which there can only be losers.

However, the boomerang effect is not restricted to risk-production zones but can be generalized to other social valuables including money, property, and legitimation. A principal effect is on property. Wherever an ecology-threatening change is made to a particular locality, such as the construction of a power station, airport or highway, property prices fall. Beck calls this ecological expropriation. The globalizing effect of ecological appropriation is progressively to make the planet uninhabitable: 'everyone is pursuing a 'scorched Earth' policy against everyone else – with resounding but seldom lasting success' (1992: 38). Equally, ecological expropriation can destroy the money-making capacities of agricultural land, forests or sea fisheries, as well as the legitimacy of corporations and governments.

At one level then, the advent of risk society reduces inequality. In particular it mitigates against class inequality because it neither respects class boundaries, nor in its afflictions establishes zero-sum relations of exploitation. In a contradictory formulation, however, Beck also argues that class disadvantage can lead to risk disadvantage, that poverty and risk attract. However, his formulation is clearly novel in that it argues for an international class system in which clean industries are retained in the economically advanced societies while dangerous and highly polluting industries are exported to the third world: 'In the shunting yard where risks are distributed, stations in 'underdeveloped provincial holes' enjoy special popularity. And one would have to be a naïve fool to continue to assume that the responsible switchmen do not know what they are doing' (1992: 41). Newly industrializing countries effectively purchase economic independence by their acceptance of risk. Here safety regulations are weak and unenforced and populations are insufficiently literate to be aware of the risks they run even where they have a choice about whether to be engaged in the risky endeavours of, say, spreading fertilizers and pesticides by hand. The managers of transnational corporations know that their capital is a necessity and that if a catastrophe should occur their resources will allow them to resist legal redress.

What they cannot resist, says Beck, is the boomerang effect and the contagion of risk: the pesticides and the toxins will return in imported foodstuffs; sulphur emissions will turn rain to acid; carbon dioxide emissions will alter the climate of the entire planet; and exported atomic power stations can melt down and emit radioactivity or their products can be used for the local construction of nuclear weapons. The boomerang effect puts the poor and the wealthy in the same neighbourhood. In his most pronounced statement of globalization Beck affirms that: 'The multiplication of risks causes the world society to contract into a community of danger' (1992: 44).

THE GLOBALIZATION PROPOSAL

Taken together, the above arguments represent a new sociology of globalization that has emerged over the past five to ten years. In summary, it proposes the following:

1 Globalization is at least contemporary with modernization and has therefore been proceeding since the sixteenth century. It involves processes of economic systematization, international relations between states, and an emerging global culture or consciousness. The process has accelerated through time and is currently in the most rapid phase of its development.

2 Globalization involves the systematic interrelationship of all the individual social ties that are established on the planet. In a fully globalized context, no given relationship or set of relationships can remain isolated or bounded. Each is linked to all the others and is systematically affected by them. This is especially true in a territorial sense (i.e. geographical boundaries in particular are unsustainable in the face of globalization). Globalization increases the inclusiveness and the unification of human society.

3 Globalization involves a phenomenology of contraction. Although commentators often speak of the shrinking of the planet or the annihilation of distance this is a phenomenological rather than a literal truth, that is, the world appears to shrink but (pretty obviously) does not materi-

ally do so. The particular phenomenological registers that alter the scalar appearance of the world are time and space. Because space tends to be measured in time[4], to the extent that the time between geographical points shortens so space appears to shrink. Insofar as the connection between physically distant points is instantaneous, space 'disappears' altogether.[5] A more recent phenomenon is that localizations of time disappear – if, for example, a Korean house-spouse can watch with an American FA–18 pilot as she bombs a chemical factory in a Middle East war, their time frames become synchronized. Globalization implies the phenomenological elimination of space and the generalization of time.

4 The phenomenology of globalization is reflexive. The inhabitants of the planet self-consciously orient themselves to the world as a whole – firms explore global markets, countercultures move from an 'alternative community' to a 'social movement' action configuration, and governments try to keep each other honest in terms of human rights and dash to commit military assistance to the maintenance of world order.

5 Globalization involves a collapse of universalism and particularism. The earlier phase of unaccelerated globalization had been characterized by a differentiation between arenas in which general and rational standards could apply and others in which the particularities of relationships and the qualities of individual persons were paramount. This differentiation is registered in the well known sociological distinctions between life chances and lifestyles, *gesellschaft* and *gemeinschaft*, public and private spheres, work and home, and system and lifeworld. The separation was largely accomplished by boundaries in time and space but because globalization annihilates time and space the distinctions can no longer apply. Each person in any relationship is simultaneously an individual and a member of the human species – they can simultaneously say 'I am myself' and 'I have rights'.

6 Globalization involves a Janus-faced mix of risk and trust. In previous eras one trusted the immediate, the knowable, the present and the material. To go beyond these was to run the risk of injury or exploitation. Under globalization individuals extend trust to unknown persons, to

impersonal forces and norms (the 'market', or 'human rights') and to patterns of symbolic exchange that appear to be beyond the control of any concrete individual or group of individuals. In so doing they place themselves in the hands of the entire set of their fellow human beings. The fiduciary commitment of all the participants is necessary for the well-being of each individual member. A fiduciary panic (e.g. the 'Black Monday' stock market crash of October 1987) creates the risk of global systemic collapse.

4

World class production: economic globalization

The working men have no country
Karl Marx

Anticipating more systematic theories of globalization, the historians contributing to the *Times Atlas of World History* (Barraclough 1978) decided that, by the middle of the twentieth century a period of European dominance had ended and the world had entered 'the age of global civilisation'. Interestingly, Barraclough reasoned that this development was economic rather than political or even cultural. Global civilization was not staked out between the emerging American and Russian superpowers nor was the world being civilized by common understandings about human rights and the environment or even decivilized by hamburgers and pop music. Rather the central events were the formation of the European Economic Community (now EU), the rise of Japan as an industrial power, and an emerging and testy confrontation between rich and poor nations. However, the key features of this world economy had been 'knitted together' between 1870 and 1914. These were threefold (Barraclough 1978: 256–7). The first was the development of transportation and communication networks that physically linked together different parts of the planet, especially by railways, shipping and the telegraph. The second was the rapid growth of trade with its accompanying pattern of dependency, especially between the relatively industrialized countries of Western Europe and the rest. The third was a huge flow of capital mainly in the form of direct investment by European firms in non-industrialized areas.

It is small wonder then that Marx developed an early theory of capitalist globalization at about this time. The capitalist seeks to transsect national boundaries extending transportation and communication into the furthest reaches of the planet, restlessly seeking to expand markets throughout the world and to appropriate ever greater tranches of labour power. Capitalism is clearly the vehicle of economic globalization because its particular institutions – financial markets, commodities, contractualized labour, alienable property – facilitate economic exchanges over great distances. For this reason, we have seen many theories of globalization take their lead from Marx in stressing its economic foundations. For these authors, as capitalism expands across the globe it internationalizes the associated pattern of social relations known as class. For some authors (e.g. Frank 1971; Wallerstein 1974, 1980; see Chapter 2) the international class system consists of struggles between states as the working class in core countries becomes 'embourgeoised' and as a third-world proletariat develops in the periphery. Others (e.g. Sklair 1990: 8) reify a global capitalist class that effectively runs the planet on its own behalf.

The following sections outline the various means by which global economic relationships are accomplished: trade, investment, production, financial exchanges, labour migration, international economic cooperation, and organizational practices. These will provide the evidence on whether claims about the development of an international class structure can be sustained.

WORLD TRADE

The original and continuing fundamental of economic globalization is trade. Trade can link together geographically distant producers and consumers, often establishing a relationship of identification as well as interdependence between them. The British taste for tea, for example, could not have been cultivated in that damp little island had it not been able to export its cheap textiles to Southern Asia, albeit to sell them in captive colonial markets, along with common law, cricket and railways. Despite the collapse of colonialism, the cultural ties remain. Equally, under current circumstances, wearing Armani fashions or grilling food on a Hibachi barbecue (itself a polyglot phrase) provides an opportunity for commonality of lifestyle across the globe. Likewise, as the political science arguments discussed in Chapter 2 suggest, the transnational relationships that are established by means of trade can undermine or at least circumvent inter-state relations.

Overall, in the period since industrialization, world trade, understood as the exchange of commodities and services between nation-states, has expanded very rapidly. One indicator is the positive ratio of growth rates in trade to growth rates in production throughout the nineteenth century and the second half of the twentieth. Only during the global conflict and associated economic depression that marked the first half of the twentieth century did that ratio turn negative. Even then global trade continued to grow except in the twenty years following the Great Depression (Gordon 1988: 43). There were two main phases of trade growth: the mid- to late nineteenth century when British military and economic hegemony allowed it to set up protected markets in its colonies and 'free trade' in manufactured goods outside them; and the thirty or so years after the Second World War when the USA was so economically and militarily dominant that it too could impose a freer trade regime, secure in the knowledge that its own manufactured exports would succeed and that it could extend special forms of trade access to its friends, those 'most favored nations.'

As Marx noticed, the great expansion of world trade began in the final quarter of the nineteenth century. Between 1800 and 1913 international trade as a proportion of world product grew from 3 to 33 per cent and it grew threefold between 1870 and 1913 (Barraclough 1978: 256). The pattern was mainly imperialistic in character. It involved the transfer of primary products from the non-industrialized world (which for most of the century mainly comprised the settler colonies of the Americas, Southern Africa and Australasia rather than the conquest colonies of Africa and Asia, India being the notable exception) in exchange for European manufactures. In 1914 only 11 per cent of world trade took place between primary producers themselves but trade between industrialized countries was growing as fast as 'imperialist' trade. Britain led the pack being the largest trading nation in mid-century but by 1900 the European states and the USA were catching up (see Figure 4.1).[1] Nevertheless, in the period up to the great depression, world trade was dominated and organized by four nation-states, Britain, France, Germany and the USA.

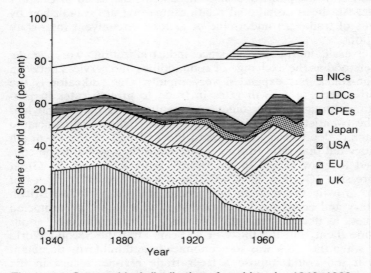

Figure 4.1 Geographical distribution of world trade, 1840–1983
Data source: Gordon 1988: 46–7

The inter-war period saw a return to protectionism as national governments strived to restore their shattered economies by curtailing imports and subsidising exports. However the emergence of the USA as the post-Second World War political, military and economic hegemon gave it an opportunity to establish a trade system that suited its interests. Insofar as much of the rest of the industrialized world had been exhausted or devastated by war, the USA was well placed to take advantage of a liberalized trade regime. The main vehicle was the General Agreement on Tariffs and Trade (GATT), an organization established by twenty-three countries in 1947. GATT has since globalized to include over one hundred members. GATT's two-pronged strategy has been to encourage members to restrict protection only to tariff duties (as opposed to quotas and subsidies) and then to seek consensus on tariff reduction. Under American encouragement, at least until about 1980, it was very successful, going through seven rounds of tariff reduction. American tariffs on industrial goods reduced from an average of 60 per cent in 1934 to 4.3 per cent in 1987, at which point Japanese industrial tariffs averaged 2.9 per cent and the EU averaged 4.7 per cent (Walters and Blake 1992: 16).

World trade grew by 6.6 per cent per annum between 1948 and 1966 and by 9.2 per cent per annum between 1966 and 1973. The critical geographical shift during this period was the relative decline of the British share of world trade, the increased trading effectiveness of the EEC (now EU), and the emergence of Japan as a trading power. Taken together the share of world trade taken by Less Developed Countries (LDCs) and Newly Industrializing Countries (NICs) improved in the 1950s and has since remained stable at 25 to 30 per cent. This has generally increased the level of global economic interdependence.

Social scientists have become accustomed to interpreting global trade relations in terms of asymmetrical dependency, for which Wallerstein (1974, 1980) offers one of the strongest arguments. However, the declining concentration of world trade in Europe and the USA and the increasing extent to which trade accounted for most national GDPs moved dependency relationships in the direction of greater symmetry during the post-war period. There was, for example, a dramatic increase in the proportion of trade in manufactured goods and most of that trade took place between industrialized countries. The proportion of the manufactured exports going from industrialized countries to other industrialized countries increased from about 30 per cent in 1935 to 64 per cent in 1983 (Gordon 1988: 47).

By most reckonings, in the 1970s and 1980s the rate of acceleration in world trade slowed. The USA could no longer count on manufacturing advantages against Japanese and European expansion and turned protectionist. Indeed the USA has met Japanese and European neomercantilism expressed as non-tariff trade barriers and production and export subsidies with similar measures of its own. During the 1980s world trade has been organized as a series of competing trade blocs (e.g. ASEAN, EU, NAFTA) that seek to remove trade barriers between members but are protectionist relative to the rest. Consequently the 'Uruguay round' of GATT negotiations, concluded in 1993, and focusing on agriculture, services and non-tariff barriers, was the most protracted and difficult of all. Nevertheless, trade has continued to grow, albeit at a slower rate.

This neomercantilist pattern might suggest that globalization in the area of trade has slowed. However, it must be remembered that the globalization proposal does not imply an absence of global conflict. In these terms, the formation and expansion of NAFTA, for example, might be seen as a globalizing strategy precisely because it is consciously directed to accomplishing economic security in an increasingly competitive global arena. It indicates that even an economy as large and powerful as that of the USA can no longer rely on its domestic market for security.

The expansion of world trade has not been lost on companies catering to mass consumer markets. Indeed, corporate executives have long been advised that: 'The globalization of markets is at hand' (Levitt 1983: 92). This expansion, like many other aspects of modernity, has become reflexive. The American fast food operator, McDonald's, for example, faces huge competition in a home market that is expanding by less than 5 per cent a year and in which it already has 90,000 outlets. The only possibility for increased profitability is globalization. This it is doing – two-thirds of the outlets it opens each year are now outside the USA where only two-thirds of all its restaurants are now located. It is also engaged in transferring its management culture to regional centres, for example, to Hong Kong for expansion into China (*The Economist* 13/11/93: 69–70).

THE INTERNATIONAL DIVISION OF LABOUR

World trade implies a division of labour between societies. Classical arguments about the division of labour consider it as an intra-societal process operating in two dimensions, the social and the technical. The social division of labour concerns the degree of specialization of jobs or occupations, the technical the degree of specialization of tasks within occupations. One of the revelatory discoveries offered by social science in the twentieth century is that colonialism and imperialism produce an international division of labour of the social kind. Core or metropolitan societies do capital-intensive, high value-adding production while peripheral societies do labour-intensive, low value-adding production. This division of labour produces a relationship of domination and mutual dependency which is self-reproducing. Thus, the customary vision of a partly globalized world is that it is fractured by a binary division variously characterized as developed/underdeveloped, modern/traditional, industrialized/industrializing, more developed/less developed, first world/third world, North/South or simply rich/poor.

The sources of this division are the trade and investment patterns discussed in the sections above. By the middle of the twentieth century these had produced an ever-widening gap between rich and poor. On an income per head basis the rich:poor ratio was about 2:1 in 1800, by 1945 it was 20:1 and by 1975 it was 40:1. In that year GDP per capita in the USA was $6,500 but there were 17 countries with a total population of 200 million living on less than $100 per year per head. Poverty is accompanied by pathological rates of literacy, life expectancy, infant mortality, nutrition, morbidity and population growth (Barraclough 1978: 294).

However, three recent globalizing effects have altered the clarity of this division: some LDCs have indeed developed very rapidly to become NICs; new forms of multinational enterprise (MNE) imply a dispersion of production tasks across the globe (see the section below) and part of this process involves the relocation of some types of manufacturing production to LDCs; and some LDCs have managed to cartelize and thus to improve returns from primary production. Taken together they indicate that the global division of labour is now proceeding on a technical as well as a social level and so we consider each of these developments in turn.

The liberal trade environment provided by the American hegemon after 1950 allowed certain LDCs to take advantage of neomercantilist policies in order to shift their position in the international division of labour. The Asian NICs (Hong Kong, Singapore, South Korea, Taiwan and latterly Malaysia and Thailand) have generally used export-oriented measures while the Latin American NICs (Brazil, Chile and Mexico) prefer import-substitution measures. Specific policy initiatives include tax incentives to investors, duty free importation of components and capital goods, wage suppression, and depressed currency values (Walters and Blake 1992: 190). So rapidly have the Asian dragons developed that they have overtaken many DMEs (developed market economies) on the usual indicator of wealth, GDP per capita. Moreover they produce sophisticated consumption items and components, often at the leading edge of technology, as well as traditional labour-intensive items such as clothing.

At the end of the following section on MNEs we note the emergence of new forms of inter-firm alliance. The spread of these arrangements in the 1980s has been little short of spectacular – by means of subcontracting, production licensing, joint ventures, partial mergers, and interfirm agreements (OECD 1992: 13–14). Many such arrangements take place between firms located in industrial societies but there is considerable evidence that some sectors of manufacturing industry are being located offshore in LDCs where they can take advantage of lower wages and taxes and more liberal labour-protection and environmental protection regimes. The OECD (1992) documents four industries that have been globalized in this way:

- Automobile parts: international trade in car parts has expanded three-fold in twenty years indicating a 'componentization' of the car industry. The key feature is Japanese expansion and its investment in the American industry; non-OECD (non-DME) countries will account for 16 per cent of global production by the year 2000 with Korea the major player.
- Chemicals: less globalized than other industries; dominated by EU and USA; non-OECD countries produce 25 per cent, about a quarter of this within transnational corporations (TNC).
- Construction: primarily a domestic industry tied to localities; dominated by EU whose share has increased to over half and the USA whose share has declined to about a quarter; Korea is the only major non-OECD contributor.
- Semiconductors (memory chips, microprocessors): highly diversified product; 90 per cent of production is by 10 TNCs; the proportion produced in the USA has declined from 60 per cent in 1978 to 34 per cent in 1988 while Japan's share has increased from 24 to 40 per cent; offshore production increased from 7 to 14 per cent in the same period (OECD 1992: 143)

Fröbel et al. (1980) offer a similar set of case studies but from the point of view of shifts in employment patterns. They find the following developments:

- German textile and garment industry: foreign employment doubled between 1966 and 1975 while domestic employment increased only a quarter; this is the result of the growth of foreign subsidiaries and subcontracting.

- German manufacturing: employs 1.5 million workers abroad, mainly in low-wage companies; this is equivalent to about 20 per cent of the domestic labour force; between 1961 and 1976 the number of foreign subsidiaries increased fourfold.
- Free production zones in NICs: in 1975 there were 79 of these zones (offering cheap labour and low taxes and regulations); concentrated in the textile and electronics industries.

The consequences of these developments can be viewed in Figure 4.2. The key development is the decline of British industrial dominance from the nineteenth century onwards. The USA and

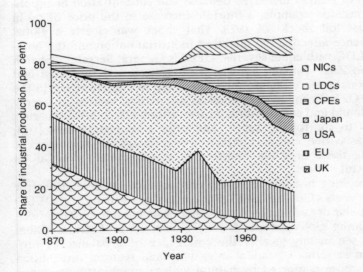

Figure 4.2 Global distribution of industrial production, 1870–1983
Data source: Gordon 1988: 32

expanded its share of world production in the twentieth century but since about 1960 its share has shrunk to nineteenth-century levels. In all then the share of industrial production in Europe the USA has contracted considerably since the Second World War in the face of expansion in Japan, the centrally planned economies (CPE), the LDCs and the NICs. At least some of this shift must be attributable to the establishment of the New International Economic Order (NIEO) in 1974 under the sponsorship of the UN Commission for Trade and Development (UNCTAD) under which industrialized states gave preference to manufactured exports from LDCs.

A particular form of neomercantilist strategy has been practised by LDCs engaged in primary production. This is the formation of producer cartels that aim to restrict production and to maintain or enhance prices. The most successful example and the model for other attempts is the Organization of Petroleum Exporting Countries (OPEC) formed in 1960 to prevent a price reduction forced by the oligopsonizing MNE cartel known as the 'seven sisters'. OPEC really became active in the 1970s, a period of sharply increased demand and concentration of supply, imposing, for example, a fourfold increase in the price of oil in the first 'oil shock' of 1973. That shock was clearly a global experience affecting the mightiest industrial nation and the humblest LDC with equal severity. OPEC's General Secretary, Sheikh Ahmed Zaki Yamani, became a recognized and respected and occasionally feared figure throughout the world. However, in the 1980s OPEC's influence waned as alternative sources of supply were found and conservation measures took effect. Similar cartels sought to control the supply and price of copper, bauxite, tin, bananas, coffee, cocoa, rubber, iron ore, phosphates and mercury. Among these only the non-ferrous metals cartels were at all successful.

Speaking broadly, there are two possible interpretations for these events (Gordon 1988). The first, promoted by the OECD and similar organizations, argues that production has indeed been undergoing globalization. A fully globalized production system would see in any locality the emergence of a balance of production in terms of capital intensivity and sectoral distribution except those conferred by natural and geographical advantages. Fröbel *et al.* present an alternative argument in favour of a 'new international division of labour' in which: 'commodity production is being split into fragments which can be assigned to whichever part of the world can provide the most profitable combination of capital and labour' (1980: 14). This new international division of labour is technical in character and it can therefore be the vehicle for a genuine globalization of production. The emergence of high levels of structural unemployment that it produces in the DMEs might be the first evidence of equalization in the international system of stratification.

We have so far concentrated on divisions of labour in the production of material commodities. However, a key feature of the contemporary period is the dematerialization of commodity production (Lash and Urry 1994), especially in the most economically advanced parts of the world that have managed to export the most labour-intensive aspects of goods production. These are experiencing the extreme effects of two processes. The first is post-industrialization (Bell 1976) in which a majority of the labour force is now engaged in the production of commodified services rather than material commodities. One group of workers thus engaged constitutes Bell's new and dominant professional and technical class, another is an urban underclass producing menial services in a context of uncertain employment. The second is the hypercommodification and industrialization of culture, what Lash and Urry call the exchange of signs for finance or what might be called an exchange of money for meanings. There is nothing particularly new about this development except that it has expanded enormously. For the moment, as the section on mass media in Chapter 6 argues, large organizations proliferate cultural products in dazzling collage of symbolized meanings.

Post-industrialization and the industrialization of culture imply the production of more mobile and easily tradeable products. Services are most often exported by mobilizing individuals as in the visit from head office, the international conference, the overseas expert, or the 'foreign' student. However they can also increasingly be exported by electronic transmission which is especially the case for financial services. Aesthetic commodities can be exported more directly, especially insofar as broadcasting technology becomes more widely available. Generally speaking, globalization will increase to the extent that world production is devoted to these non-material commodities precisely because they are so mobile.

MULTINATIONAL ENTERPRISES

The main focus for many hopes and fears about economic globalization is the MNE or TNC. For critics of capitalism they are the vehicles by which intolerable and inhuman practices of exploitation are spread across the globe, and for its friends they are the virtuous sources of investment, technology transfer and the upgrading of the labour force. Until recently it was also possible to offer the more moderate critique of MNEs that they had grown so large and powerful that they undermined the legitimate and often democratically established sovereign authority of the nation-state but in the current context of the delegitimation of the state the debate has become polarized.

Among critics, MNEs tend to be theorized rather than to be defined operationally – Sklair (1991) for example gives no definition of a TNC. By contrast, Dunning, who is more friend than enemy, defines an MNE as: 'an enterprise that engages in FDI [foreign direct investment] and organizes the production of goods or services in more than one country' (1993: 6). However, Dunning stresses that this definition cannot capture the extent to which transnational activities can vary in their scope and intensiveness. They vary their multinational engagement according to: the number of subsidiaries; the number of countries; the proportion of activities accounted for by foreign activities; the degree to which ownership and management are internationalized; the extent to which central administrative and research activities are internationalized; and the balance of advantages and disadvantages to the countries in which they operate. A classical example of a 'villainous' MNE might be General Motors but only about a third of its assets and a third of its sales are outside the USA (and most of these are in first-world Canada, Europe and Australia). Perhaps a more appropriate example of a 'true' multinational might be the Swiss-Swedish engineering group, Asea Brown Boveri or the Dutch Electronics firm, Philips, each of which have over 85 per cent of their sales outside their country of origin (data from Emmott 1993: 6).

We can now consider the general extent of MNE activity in the global economy. Dunning (1993: 14–15) estimates that in 1988 there were about 20,000 MNEs with foreign assets amounting to $1.1 trillion (equivalent to 8 per cent of gross world product) and total assets of over $4 trillion. They accounted for: 25–30 per cent of combined GDP in all market economies; 75 per cent of international commodity trade; and 80 per cent of international exchanges of technology and managerial skills. The largest 300 MNEs account for 70 per cent of total FDI and 25 per cent of the world's capital (Dunning 1993: 15; Emmott 1993: 6). Overall, FDI increased fourfold between 1970 and 1990 but most of this increase has occurred during the late 1980s (Emmott 1993: 8). Over 90 per cent of FDI is sourced in ten developed countries, and about two-thirds originated in only four (USA, UK, Japan, Germany). However, MNEs are themselves becoming internationalized, insofar as these rates have declined over the past 20 years.

There is a significant increase in the number of MNEs originating in the developing societies, the oil-producing countries, and the Asian dragons (NICs). For example, the Asian share of FDI rose from 3.6 per cent in 1973 to 9.3 per cent in 1988 (Dunning 1993: 21). The destinations of FDI largely match the sources, and indeed: 'there appears to be a growing symmetry between outward and inward foreign capital stake in the case of most [individual] countries' (Dunning 1993: 24). This must give at least some pause for thought to critics who insist that MNEs are the trojan horse for first-world economic domination of the third world.

The combined effects of these trends allow Dunning (1993: 40) to identify a series of what he describes as true global industries, those that are dominated by large corporations of diverse national origins, producing and marketing in all of the world's largest economies. The most important example is the petrochemical industry but others, in descending order of importance, include cars, consumer electronics, tyres, pharmaceuticals, tobacco, soft drinks, fast food, financial consultancies, and luxury hotels. We can add to this list emerging multinational alliances (which normally involve much lower levels of FDI but high levels of managerial coordination) in airlines, telecommunications, and banking and insurance.

As in the case of many of the components of globalization, the development of MNEs is a long-term process with a recent acceleration rather than a sudden and qualitative shift. This development is traced through several phases by Dunning (1993: 96–136; also see Gilpin 1987: 238–45):

- Mercantile capitalism and colonialism (1500–1800): exploitation of natural resources and agriculture in colonized regions by state-sponsored, chartered companies (e.g. Dutch East India, Hudson's Bay, Massachusetts Bay, Muscovy, and Van Diemen's Land Companies).
- Entrepreneurial and financial capitalism (1800–75): embryonic development of control of supplier and consumer

markets by acquisition; infrastructural investment by finance houses in transportation and construction.
* International capitalism (1875–1945): rapid expansion of resource-based and market-seeking investments; growth of American-based international cartels.
* Multinational capitalism (1945–60): American domination of FDI; expanded economic imperialism; expansion in scale of individual MNEs.
* Globalizing capitalism (1960–90): shift from resource-based and market-seeking investment to spatial optimization of production and profit opportunities; growth of European and Japanese sourced FDI; increased FDI in the European ex-state socialist societies; expansion of inter-firm alliances and joint ventures; increased offshore outsourcing of components.

The extent to which the latest phase represents a globalizing shift or acceleration is indicated by Gilpin:

> These developments foretell the end of the old multi-nationalism. The day is passed when corporations of the United States and a few other developed countries could operate freely in and even dominate the host economies and when foreign direct investment meant the ownership and control of wholly owned subsidiaries. Instead, a great variety of negotiated arrangements have been put in place: cross-licensing of technology among corporations of different nationalities, joint ventures, orderly marketing agreements, secondary sourcing, off-shore production of components, and crosscutting equity ownership. In the developed countries the General Motors-Toyota alliance is undoubtedly a harbinger of things to come. In the developing world the corporations see the LDCs less as pliable exporters of raw materials and more as expanding local markets and industrial partners or even potential rivals. Thus the relatively simple models of both liberal [modernization] and dependency theorists are becoming outmoded in the final quarter of the century.
>
> (Gilpin 1987: 256)

Data on these new forms of MNE that may or may not require direct investment are scarce but all observers appear to agree that they are developing much more rapidly than traditional

TNCs. The reason appears to be that the cost advantages of TNCs have met their limits. Complex companies, producing wide ranges of products in multiple markets are extremely difficult and costly to manage and to service. For this reason traditional TNCs are tending to remain regional rather than global (Emmott 1993). There is an emerging triad of overseas investors each with its own regional specialization based on propinquity and imperial history: American firms tend to invest in Latin America and some parts of Southern Asia; Europeans in Africa, Brazil, Southern Asia and Eastern Europe; and Japanese firms dominate investment in East Asia and Australasia.

The emerging form of MNE is therefore not a TNC but an 'alliance', an arrangement between firms that may involve equity swaps, technology transfers, production licensing, the division of component manufacture and assembly, market sharing, or 'rebadging'.[2] Because there is no agency that collects statistics on alliances their precise extent is impossible to assess but they are as Emmott (1993: 15) suggests a 'hot topic' in the business schools and the popular business literature. While they might be expected in the transport industry. Forming a 'global alliance' appears to be the survival strategy for any national airline, e.g. British-USAir-TAT-Deutsche BA-QANTAS-Air NZ, KLM-Northwest, Air France-Sabena-CSA, Swissair-Delta-Singapore, or telecommunications firm, e.g. Worldsource (AT&T-Kokusai Denshin Denwa-Singapore Telecom), BT-MCI, Deutsche Bundespost Telekom-France Télécom. But they also occur in unexpected quarters. IBM, for example, once manufactured mainframe computers alone but its famous PC was developed in conjunction with Microsoft, Intel and Lotus and it is now even cooperating with Apple to develop a common software architecture (Emmott 1993: 15). Indeed alliances tend to be common in smaller postindustrial or postmodernized firms at the leading edge of scientific application including information technology, new materials technology and information technology. This may be because innovation in these areas occurs on such a broad front that firms must cooperate or be left behind. International inter-firm agreements on research cooperation among semiconductor firms, for example, grew from forty-three in 1983 to over one hundred in 1989 (OECD 1992: 14).

Although these transnational *Keiretsu* might conceivably be hailed as the future, globalized shape of world business organization, a truly globalized system might look quite different. We consider in an earlier section the liberalization of world trade. Emmott (1993: 8) argues that in a completely liberalized trade environment and where the marginal costs of transportation are low, MNEs would cease to exist. This is because firms would obtain the best cost advantage by producing in one place so as to maximize economies of scale and licensing offshore production where such economies failed to offset transportation costs. In a truly globalized economic context then, the MNE would disappear in favour of local producers marketing globally.

ORGANIZATIONAL ECUMENISM

In the years just after the turn of the century many American industrial organizations went through a famous transformation. The Ford Motor Company of the USA invented the moving assembly line and thus established an ideological paradigm for economic organizations that recently has come to be called Fordism. Fordism advocates the mass production of standardized items for mass markets made affluent by high incomes. It aims to reduce the cost per item by intensive mechanization and by economies of scale in the utilization of capital equipment. Fordism became the idealized system of production not only in the capitalist West but in the socialist East.[3] Insofar as Fordism was exported by MNEs and insofar as it was mimicked, it became a major feature of the global economy in the period just after the Second World War. However, Fordism owed its success not to its capacity to produce and market goods on a wide scale but to its social and political consequences. It was an extraordinarily effective means both of controlling the labour process and of satisfying workers' aspirations at a material level. In the terms of a well-known formulation it turned proletarians into instrumental workers.

But Fordism is not a complete paradigm. In particular it leaves untouched the vast issue of who makes decisions and by what processes. In many instances this issue was resolved in terms of a parallel paradigm of work called Taylorism (after the engineer F. W. Taylor who invented it), which specified a radical differentiation between the functions of management and labour. However, Taylorism did not achieve the global impact of Fordism, partly because it was challenged by a humanistic though equally manipulative paradigm called 'human relations'. Industrial organizations could therefore vary across societies according both to the pattern of state action in regulating, coordinating, subsidizing and socializing the economy, and to cultural prescriptions of appropriate economic behaviour (see Lash and Urry 1987). So, for example: in the USA large companies were run by ex-engineers making highly rationalized technical decisions in relation to technology and markets; in Germany firms were organized and influenced jointly by state managers and finance houses; in France, large firms were centralized, state-managed bureaucracies; in Britain there was a concentration on the maintenance of the managerial status group, at the possible expense of relative industrial effectiveness; and in Scandinavia there was a deliberate effort to dedifferentiate managers and workers.

Under the current acceleration of globalization these cultural differences are tending to be subsumed within a single idealization of appropriate organizational behaviour. This paradigm incorporates many of the ideas found in preceding versions but is constructed in terms of a single, newly recognized imperative – that an organization must have the capacity to make a flexible response to uncertain market conditions caused by commodity saturation. Such an organization might be described as postmodern because it is both internally and externally hyper- or dedifferentiated.[4] Internally management and workers shade into each other in an emerging professionalized work role; externally, organizations that can adapt rapidly to changing markets will have a 'shapelessness' and individuality that makes them appear structurally similar.

There are two main alternative explanations for the shift, what might be called the postmodernization and the globalization explanations. The first, best represented in Harvey (1989), is Marxisant in its orientation, suggesting that capitalism moves in boom and bust cycles based on a pattern of capital investment–labour economies–unemployment–reduced demand–push for efficiency–further investment. These cycles build towards periodic points of 'overaccumulation' in which large amounts of capital and labour sit unused. This is manifested in a crisis of unemployment, market gluts, spare industrial capacity, and unsold inventories (Harvey 1989: 180–1) that force a radical restructuring of capitalist accumulation. The crisis of the great depression of the 1930s opened a generalized transition to Fordism and Keynesianism. A similar crisis also occurred in about 1973 when Fordist productivity so outstripped demand that a new paradigm had to be sought that would reduce market dependency.

The globalization explanation for the shift (e.g. Marceau 1992) offers a more prosaic alternative – the explanatory factor is the impressive global success of Japanese industry in challenging American and European domination. This was in part accomplished by the effectiveness of the Japanese state in coordinating industrial strategy and of the new information and material technologies that were applied to production. However, the critical factor in Japanese industrial success is a novel combination of managerial practices. These were globalized partly by the activities of Japanese MNEs, which transplanted them into branch operations outside Japan with considerable success. Local competitors have deliberately sought to match the efficiency advantages of Japanese organizational practices.[5] More importantly there has been a process of global cultural transmission in which the Japanese version of the best way has been carried around the world as a system of ideas. This transmission occurs in three arenas: in the popular mass media Japanese production systems are represented as a highly generalized but somewhat ambivalent ideal, discussed in terms of both fear and admiration; in universities, business school academics and organization theorists conduct comparative research on the Japanese advantage and these results are both published and incorporated into organizational design courses for potential managers; and third they are written up as easily digestible popular books that can be peddled to managers as manuals for organizational transformation.

We can now consider the elements of the Japanized organizational paradigm that specifies flexible specialization and accumulation, sometimes known as Toyotism (Dohse *et al*. 1985).[6] The general orientation of the paradigm is that the firm must become organization-oriented rather than being accountancy-oriented (Dore 1989), focusing on asset building and market share rather than on immediately calculated issues of cost and revenue. These elements are as follows:

1 *Strategic management*: Strategic management practices aim to forecast and, if possible, to control the future relationship between the organization and its supplier and customer markets. A typical example is the way in which prices are set low early in the production life of an item in order to secure a market share of sufficient scale in the future to maximize not merely bottom-line profitability but overall gross profits (Swyngedouw 1987: 491–3).

Another example is the practice of paying prices for raw materials at above current market defined levels in order to secure long-term supply contracts.

2 *Just-in-time (JIT)*: The basic principle of JIT is to minimize inventory at each stage of the production process since surplus inventory represents unrealized value. The production process is divided into a number of stages each organized as a team of workers. Each stage uses components on a 'go and get' basis and produces its own components on the basis of demand from the succeeding assembly stage (Swyngedouw 1987: 494–6; Wilkinson *et al.* 1992). This may be compared with the Fordist 'just in case' approach in which parts and finished products are stockpiled. An important consequence is that control over workers must be established by alternative means than those given in the flow of an assembly line, including long-term incentives to continuous worker loyalty in terms of job security, promotion possibilities and family welfare. JIT implies multiskilling, so that surplus labour time can be employed, and localized decision-making about which parts, requirements and production.

3 *Total quality management*: JIT implies that supplies of components both from outside and inside the firm must be reliable in quantity and high in quality. The Japanese quality control system depends on all workers being involved in the maintenance of production standards. Workers meet in quality control circles (QCC) where they are provided with charts and diagrams which identify systematic, as opposed to unique sources of quality failure. QCCs diffused rapidly throughout Japanese industry since the 1960s and are now spreading with similar rapidity in Europe and North America.[7]

4 *Teamwork*: The imperatives of JIT and QCCs encouraged Japanese businesses to adopt the idea of autonomous work groups developed by the British Tavistock Institute in the 1950s and 1960s. Teamwork experiments were also common throughout Europe during the 1960s and 1970s, especially in Scandinavia. Teamwork involves the collectivizing and sharing of tasks for a small group of workers at a similar stage of the production process. In some instances tasks are mixed so that distinctions between

skilled and unskilled work are broken down, in others workers maintain their individual skills but work together.

5 *Managerial decentralization*: This involves the displacement of inflexible, centrally controlled, multilayered hierarchies in favour of a shapeless and flowing matrix of shifting and flexible exchanges, a federation of organizational styles and practices each surviving on their capacity to respond to demand. The extreme form of such a structure occurs where flexibility is externalized, that is where the production of components, workers' skills and other assets is subcontracted outside the organization.[8] The contracting organization typically uses advanced technology, is large in the scale of its production, and employs highly paid, multiskilled, highly committed workers, while subcontractors are smaller in scale and employ low-paid, frequently marginal labour.[9] The constellation of subcontracted firms cushions the core firm against market shock especially where this requires labour redundancy.

6 *A numerically flexible labour force*: The chief object of numerical flexibility is the possibility of laying off labour in market downturns or periods of lack of market success and of taking it back on when demand rises. The mechanisms include part-time and temporary work, outworking, and homeworking as well as subcontracting.

7 *Functionally flexible workers*: This involves three elements: task integration which involves a widening of job classifications, task rotation and, more importantly, the involvement of manual workers in some policy implementation and conceptualizing processes; multiskilling which involves the development of broad-based skills, including both quality control and maintenance functions as well as direct operation of manufacturing equipment; localized responsibility in which middle-management functions are reappropriated by workers (Mathews 1989: 108–9).

The Japanization of organizational practices has had the important effect of culturalizing economic life. Under a liberal, nineteenth-century *laissez-faire* regime workers in organizations were regarded simply as motivated by the calculation of individual costs and benefits. As they began really to do their calculations and to realize the power provided by the possibility

of the withdrawal of their labour, firms engaged in Fordist practices of maximum control by bureaucratic and technological
means. The Japanese discovery is that this can only provide an
organization with minimal performance in relation to rules. In
order to develop a proactive commitment by workers one needs
to develop a totalizing cultural environment that gives them a
sense of belonging to a primary social group. This involves not
only the security and material benefits of 'lifetime employment'
but a reflexive attempt to reconstitute the firm as a quasi-familial
community. Part of this discovery, as is indicated above, is the
coherence of such a community depends on restricting it only to
those whose skills are absolutely necessary to the organization.

The culturalization of economic life exhibits a triple effectivity in relation to globalization. First, it is a reflexive process in
which employers deliberately gaze on their firms with the inten-
tion of providing a particular culture. They pay attention to their
employees seeking to involve them in a sense of shared belonging;
they develop corporate symbols and rituals that heighten
emotional engagement; they seek to develop the skills and abilities of their workers through training; they try to communicate
directly with employees as much as is possible rather than having
their communications mediated through a hierarchy (Thompson
and McHugh 1990: 228–31). In a reifying formulation that might
look a little odd to a sociologist, firms are classified as having
'strong' or 'weak' organizational cultures.[10] In seeking to
develop strong cultures, firms become receptive to ideas and seek
them out. Global flows of business ideas have therefore increased
very rapidly. This provides the second effect which is that the very
act of looking outside the company and outside the nation for
ideas encourages a consciousness of global events and consequences. When organization was determined by technology,
managers could believe that their firms were shaped by local
events – they no longer can. The third globalizing effect is that
Fordism in its purest form was restricted to particular types of
organization, business firms employing technologically sophisticated, large-scale capital equipment. Only here could the formula
of technological control of workers plus high wages succeed. The
new organizational paradigm can be operated in any enterprise
and indeed can be exported beyond the business sector to other
types of organization. Now not only firms but government agencies, churches, schools, hospitals, social clubs and, *horrible dictu*,
universities can all exhibit the full panoply of symbolic trappings

from the new cultural paradigm – mission statements, strategic plans, total quality management, multiskilling and staff development. This constitutes globalization not only in its recent meaning of planetary inclusion but also in its older one of totalization.

FLOATING FINANCE

Among the dimensions of economic life being considered in this chapter possibly the most globalized are the markets for raising loans and capital. These markets have a long history of internationalization. Many point to the 'Black Monday' stock market crash of October 1987 as convincing evidence of a globalized effect. Indeed, that fall in share prices globalized very rapidly. However, the planetary effects of the Wall Street crash of 1929 were far more serious if less rapid in their dispersal.

Gilpin (1987: 308–14) identifies three eras in the development of international financial markets:

- 1870–1914: Britain was the major capital exporter and international finance therefore centred on the City of London. Here foreign holdings increased fivefold in the period. The City managed the world financial system.
- 1920–39: The First World War forced many European governments, including the British, to liquidate overseas investments. Simultaneously the USA was becoming a powerful economic player. Until 1929 the USA provided liquid funds to the financial system but curtailed foreign lending in that year. Thereafter markets remained illiquid until the Second World War.
- 1947–85: New York became the international financial centre, that is, the clearing house, the banker for foreign reserves, the main capital market, and the lender-of-last-resort. American financial management was accomplished via the World Bank and the International Monetary Fund (IMF) and governmental international aid rose to equal prominence with private capital as a source of finance.

Nominally the global financial system was thus internationalized and subjected to collective fiscal management. In the post-Second World War period, the key treaty in the so-called Bretton Woods Agreement of 1944 established the IMF. The IMF's brief was to maintain stability in rates of currency exchange by providing temporary loans to carry states through periodic balance-of-payments deficits without massive structural readjustment. For some 25 years the IMF thus effectively returned American balance-of-payments surpluses to countries in deficit, although in chronic instances it did demand readjustment, and in many cases states simply went ahead and devalued. An important stabilizing factor was the linking of the value of the dollar to a specific price of gold.

Although highly internationalized, neither the pre-war nor the post-war system was fully globalized because each depended on centralized management and underwriting by a single state. The London system had failed to function in the 1930s when no government was prepared to underwrite it and a similar crisis occurred in the early 1970s. The key source of the crisis was the relative decline of American industrial and trading power (discussed above). Several factors contributed to the American decline – the rise of regional trading blocs, the emergence of Japan and the NICs, and the OPEC oil shock. The USA became a debtor rather than a creditor nation and began to finance its debt by pumping dollars into the market at just about the same time as the OPEC nations were doing the same with their dollar-denominated surpluses. Many of these liquid funds found a home in the LDCs which ran up uncontrollable levels of debt. More importantly, a market for American dollars, known as the Euro-dollar or Eurocurrency market, developed beyond the managerial reach of New York. This globalized 'stateless' money increased in volume from $50 billion in 1973 to $2 trillion in 1987, almost the same as the amount circulating in the USA itself (Harvey 1989: 163).

The key event that signalled the collapse of the Bretton Woods system was the withdrawal of the US dollar from the gold standard because the relationship could no longer be maintained in the face of dollar inflation. Already the IMF had supplemented gold by so-called Special Drawing Rights (SDRs), the rights to borrow from the IMF as necessary, as the fiduciary support for the dollar and other currencies. Now SDRs have replaced gold, sterling and the US dollar as the global standard of accounting and are constituted as a weighted mix of five currencies ($US, £Stg, DM, FFr, ¥). However, the SDR has not become global currency.

In a non-globalized system one would have expected a shift of the financial centre, perhaps to Frankfurt or Tokyo, but this did not happen. Rather, a genuine globalization process has occurred so that location is no longer relevant. This 'fourth era' has emerged from the coincidence between the decline of New York and the development of instantaneous and computerized telecommunications. The global financial market has developed in two directions. First, the elimination of space has accomplished the conquest of time. Because the opening times in particular localities overlap, twenty-four hour trading by electronic access has been made possible, and arbitrage much more technical and frantic. This continuous trading extends to dealing in currency, stocks, securities, futures, and commodities. Second, financial markets have dedifferentiated so that banks have become stockdealers, building societies and credit unions have become banks and so on. The relevance of this postmodernizing effect to the present argument is that the entire system has become more difficult to control. States are placed at the mercy of financial markets – the collapse of the European Monetary System in 1992 was the consequence of persistent market attacks on its weaker elements, for example. All the power of the Bundesbank could not save it.

The only way in which governments can affect financial markets is by intervening in them rather than regulating them or by collectively underwriting currencies. They often attempt to do this on a concerted basis with occasional success, as in 1985 when the seven largest economies persuaded the markets to devalue the dollar by selling tranches of their holdings, but with frequent failure, as in 1987 when they bought 90 billion dollars but failed to protect the currency's value. The political leaders of the seven largest economies (G7) and their central bankers do meet on a regular basis with a view to aligning their domestic economic policies and smoothing the effects of trade imbalances. In general this usually means putting pressure on Germany and Japan to reduce trade surpluses and this is the current extent of global financial management.

The globalization of financial markets affects individuals as well as states. Its effect in linking distant localities is well captured in the following description:

> Banking is rapidly becoming indifferent to the constraints of time, place and currency.... an English buyer can get a Japanese mortgage, an American can tap his New York bank account through a cash machine in Hong Kong and a Japanese investor can buy shares in a London-based

Scandinavian bank whose stock is denominated in sterling, dollars, Deutsche Marks and Swiss francs.
(*Financial Times* 8/5/78, cited in Harvey 1989: 161)

Their effect in globalizing culture and consciousness must therefore be equally profound.

MIGRANT LABOUR

If among factor exchange systems financial markets are the most globalized, labour markets are the least so. No other area of economic life remains so much under the thrall of states and so resistant to globalizing effects. This is possibly because governments remain accountable to electorates in terms of the delivery of individual economic welfare and the admission of migrants appears to threaten employment prospects and to dilute the value of public services. And while government prohibition is the major constraint on labour mobility it is not the only one. Members of the EU have the right to live and work anywhere within the Union, for example, but internal migration has been minimal despite internal variations in living standards (Emmott 1993: 6). It would appear that only quite severe economic or political disadvantage can overcome the local constraints of kin, language, domestic investments and cultural familiarity.

In fact, the earliest stages of global expansion saw the highest levels of labour mobility. In its initial phase much of this mobility was incontravertibly forced. Between 1500 and 1850 white traders moved 9.5 million slaves from Africa to the Americas, including 4 million to the Caribbean, 3.5 million to Brazil and another 400,000 to the Southern USA. The forced convict settlement of Australia and America, although almost as harsh, affected much lower numbers (McEvedy and Jones 1978: 277). Until 1800 'free' white settler colonization was relatively slight – up to that year less than a million Europeans had crossed the Atlantic. The nineteenth century saw the 'Great Migration'. Between 1845 and 1914, 41 million people migrated to the Americas, mainly from Europe and mainly to the USA (McEvedy and Jones 1978: 279). After the First World War the USA placed restrictions on the number of immigrants but it continues to absorb relatively large numbers. It has received 600,000 per year in the past five years (Emmott 1993: 7).

American immigration restrictions in the twentieth century

diverted much European migration to the former British settler colonies of Australia, Canada, New Zealand and South Africa, Australasia having received a total of 5.5 million migrants (McEvedy and Jones 1978: 325). A huge proportion of these migrants moved on the basis of purely economic motivations. However, this mass migration pattern no longer applies. Following the economic crises that began in around 1970 most of the societies that previously had been 'open' placed numerical and qualification restrictions on immigration.

Since the Second World War the main patterns of international migration have been as follows (see Cohen 1987):

- Continued European and Asian settler migration to North America, Australasia and Southern Africa.
- Post-Vietnam war refugee migration.
- Latin-American migration to the USA mainly from Cuba, Mexico and Puerto Rico.
- Return migration from ex-colonies to the European 'mother countries', especially to Britain (from black Africa, South Asia and the West Indies), France (from North Africa), the Netherlands (from Indonesia) and Portugal (from Africa).
- *Gästarbeiter* 'temporary' migration from Southern Europe (mainly Turkey and ex-Yugoslavia) into the booming economies of Northern Europe (especially Western Germany and Switzerland).
- 'Temporary' migration of Asians to the oil-exporting countries of the middle East and to Japan.
- Jewish migration to Israel, especially from Russia and Eastern Europe.
- East European migration to Western Europe and the USA (Western Germany, for example, has been receiving 440,000 immigrants per year for five years) (Emmot 1992: 7)

These developments are patchy and by no means represent a globalized picture. In a genuinely globalized market, movements of labour and patterns of settlement would be entirely unrestricted by states. However, there are some inklings of evidence that, even here the powers of nation-states may be waning. If they are numerous enough, individual decisions can overwhelm the regulative practices of even the most draconian preventative measures. Several events bear witness to this: the mass 'illegal' migration of Mexicans into the USA; successful migrations by

Indo-Chinese 'boat people'; the collapse of the barbed-wire frontier between Eastern and Western Europe; the student migration from China following the Tiananmen Square massacre in 1989; and the determination of European *Gästarbeiter* to achieve full citizenship rights even in the face of violent racial assaults. As global consciousness increases, so too will the pressures in favour of a single labour and settlement market.

TRANSNATIONAL CLASSES

Traditional views of class focus on the nation-state-society-economy as the object of class action. In Marxist analyses, classes struggle for the control and eventual abolition of the state. Indeed, as we saw in Chapter 1, Marx envisioned true globalization as the outcome of proletarian revolutionary success. Similarly, in Weberian analyses, classes struggle at the state level about the distribution of rewards in society. If one accepts the veracity of class analysis then classes must be specified as nationalized collective actors. We must therefore now ask whether classes can continue to exist under two sets of conditions that might be seen as having a decomposing effect on them. The first is the decline of the state, discussed in Chapter 5, that removes the prize, the object of the struggle. The second is the marketization and globalization of the international economy that may be depriving classes of an arena in which to struggle. In a global economic market that has no centre there might be no place in which classes can confront one another.

The strongest claim that the class struggle has simply moved up a notch from the national to the international level is made by such authors as Van der Pijl (1989). Van der Pijl argues that as globalization proceeds the capitalist class transforms itself in an international direction in three moments:

- it develops an international class consciousness – this occurs relatively early within, for example, Grotius' concepts of international law, and Kant's postulation of the need for a world state;
- it develops a controlling state-like structure at the international level – this can be witnessed in the League of Nations and the United Nations which, armoured by American power, made the world safe for capitalism;
- it socializes labour in order to demarcate an international

economic space – this is accomplished by the internationalization of trade, investment and production that
divides the world into exploiting and exploited states.

These provide the conditions for the development of an informal
international capitalist class that consists of a network of big
companies linked together by interlocking directorates and cross-
shareholdings. These, plus such organizations as the UN, allow
this class to manage an international division of labour in such a
way as to allow the bourgeoisie to maintain its position in the
core societies by exporting poverty.

The analysis of globalization processes presented throughout
this book would tend to deny the possibility of the internationalization of class, at least insofar as it is represented in such vulgar
formulations as this. The following arguments apply: there cannot
be a ruling class without a state and the UN scarcely qualifies as
a world state; internal social divisions of labour are tending to
dedifferentiate so that the functions of conceptualization and
execution are tending to be reintegrated; firms are downscaling
so that core large firms will decreasingly be able to dominate the
system; markets are becoming tokenized and decentred so that
they are becoming increasingly difficult to control; and the key
means of production are no longer physical plant and machines
but human expertise, symbolized information and aesthetic
products, each of which is ephemeral, non-accumulable and
uncontrollable. This does not mean that the global economy is
without its powerful individual movers and shakers. It is impossible to deny the impact of a Rupert Murdoch or George Soros,[11]
or that Silvio Berlusconi succeeded where Ross Perot failed.
However, they are powerful precisely because of their individual
talents and not because they are the members of a class. Indeed
in a more unpredictable global economy, individual success might
be viewed as precarious without class support – *vide* Alan Bond
or Donald Trump.

This is not to suggest, however, that economic stratification
has disappeared from the face of the earth. Rather, that the
stratification pattern is now focused on possibilities for consumption rather than production relations. The emerging pattern is
indeed an international one, in which members of rich societies,
even if they are unemployed, tend to enjoy significantly better
consumption possibilities than employees in developing societies.
This has been apparent for some time but a significant feature of

the current acceleration is the way in which the two worlds are beginning to mingle in global cities. Lash and Urry (1994) identify a new configuration that juxtaposes an affluent post-industrial service class or middle mass in high-paying relatively autonomous occupations with a disadvantaged *Gästarbeiter* class or underclass that supports its consumption within routine underpaid and insecure labour situations. Under globalization, migration has brought the third world back to the global cities where its exploitation becomes ever more apparent.

A GLOBALIZED ECONOMY?

We are now in a position, as in each of these three substantive chapters, to take stock of the process of globalization in each of the dimensions we have isolated. Table 4.1 sets out two columns. On the left is an ideal-typical configuration of a globalized economy, on the right an inventory of approximations to the components of the ideal type. Globalization is most advanced in the areas of financial markets and organizational ideologies and least advanced in the labour market. A critical differentiating factor here appears to be mediation. Both financial markets and ideological arenas are highly 'tokenized', that is the exchanges within them are symbolically mediated. Similarly there is considerable and increasing symbolic mediation in the arenas of trade and investment particularly insofar as services are becoming an increasing component of trade and as information and human skills become constituted as capital. At the risk of subscribing to the hacker reification, 'information wants to be free', symbolic goods cannot be constrained within geographical and temporal boundaries in the way that material items can. Labour, on the other hand, remains resolutely material and largely controllable and so this market remains subject to the regulation of individual preferences.

This argument can lead us back to an element of the paradigmatic proposal of this book. As is indicated in the Introduction, speaking roughly, the theorem that underlies it is that material relationships localize (*pace* Marx and Wallerstein), power relationships internationalize, and symbolic relationships globalize. As a given sector of social life moves from a predominance of material through power through symbolic relationships, the tendency will be towards globalization. In each of the dimensions of economic life we have inspected we can identify an

Table 4.1 An inventory of economic globalization

Dimension	Ideal-typical pattern of globalization	Current state of affairs
Trade	Absolute freedom of exchange between localities. Indeterminate flows of services and symbolic commodities.	Minimum tariff barriers. Substantial non-tariff and cultural barriers. Regional neomercantilism.
Production	Balance of production activity in any locality determined only by physical/ geographical advantages.	International social division of labour being displaced by a technical division of labour. Substantial decentralization of production. Dematerialization of commodities
Investment	Minimal FDI. Displaced by trade and production alliances.	TNCs being displaced by alliance arrangements but considerable FDI remains.
Organizational ideology	Flexible responsiveness to global markets.	Flexibility paradigm has become orthodox but very substantial sectors of Fordist *practice* remain.
Financial market	Decentralized, instantaneous and 'stateless'	Globalization largely accomplished.
Labour market	Free movement of labour. No permanent identification with locality.	Increasingly state regulated. Considerable individual pressure for opportunities for 'economic' migration.

approximate periodization of modern society that corresponds with this theorem. Between about 1600 and 1870 we find a period of 'capitalist economy', fading absolutist empires and emerging but weak nation-states. Trans-geographical links are established by entrepreneurial traders and merchants. Between about 1870 and 1970 we find a 'political economy', a system of international or more precisely inter-organizational economic relations. The power of a state depends on the strength of its economy, on the capacity of its national enterprises to trade and invest and become multinational. States collaborate with MNEs to enhance their economies in the international system by steering flows of labour, trade and investment. Emergent hegemons can manage the international financial system through nominally international organizations.

The inhabitants of the planet now appear to have entered a third phase, a phase of 'cultural economy'. Here symbolicized markets move beyond the capacity of states to manage them and units of economic production start to downscale to a more individual and humanized scale. The economy becomes so subordinate to individual taste and choice that it becomes reflexively marketized and, because tokenized systems do not succumb to physical boundaries, reflexively globalized. The leading sectors in this process are those whose commodities are themselves symbols, the mass media and entertainment industries and the post-industrialized service industries (Lash and Urry 1994). The economy can thus turn on and penetrate the remaining defences of economic and political geography. It also follows that in a culturalized global economy, world class is displaced by a world status system based on consumption, lifestyle and value-commitment.

5

Earthly powers: political globalization

The nation-state is becoming too small for the big problems of life, and too big for the small problems of life
Daniel Bell

The preceding chapter indicates that in many material dimensions there is an increasing interconnectedness and interdependence between the constituent economic units of formerly separate societies. Inter-societal exchanges of management, capital, components, finance, labour and commodities are increasing relative to intra-societal exchanges. In Chapter 2 we examine the way in which the disciplines of political science and international relations have sought to theorize the impact of these and other changes. It will be remembered that typically they theorize the world in dualistic terms – the world is argued to be globalizing at the level of economics and culture but states remain the primary location for sovereignty and decision-making. In this chapter we can examine a radical counter-proposal, the argument that the state too is affected by globalization and that political activity increasingly focuses on cross-societal issues.

The best and most explicit outline of the general argument is given by Held (1991: 207–9). He begins at the level of non-political, inter-societal connections and then takes the argument through a series of steps which see the undermining of the nation-state and its eventual displacement by a world government. The steps in Held's argument are as follows:

- Increasing economic and cultural connections reduce the power and effectiveness of governments at the nation-state level – they can no longer control the flow of ideas and economic items at their borders and thus their internal policy instruments become ineffective.
- State power is further reduced because transnational processes grow in scale as well as in number – TNCs for example are often larger and more powerful than many governments.
- Many traditional areas of state responsibility (e.g. defence, communications, economic management) must therefore be coordinated on an international or intergovernmental basis.
- States have thus been obliged to surrender sovereignty within larger political units (e.g. EU, ASEAN), multilateral treaties (e.g. NATO, OPEC), or international organizations (e.g. UN, WTO (GATT), IMF).
- A system of 'global governance' is therefore emerging with its own policy development and administrative systems which further curtails state power.
- This provides the basis for the emergence of a supranational state with dominant coercive and legislative power.

The critical point of debate is the issue of how far the world has gone and will go within the last three steps. For many 'realists' (e.g. McGrew 1992b) the prevailing territorial sovereignty of nation-states and the meaning they have for their citizens makes them the undeniably primary context of political life. For 'modernists' such as Held the sovereignty of the state is already in decline and 'world government', although not taking the same form as contemporary nation-state governments, is a real possibility. As might be expected on the basis of the previous chapters, this book veers towards the second of these positions.

Before making a case in that direction, however, it is worth reiterating a point made by Giddens (1985) and stressed by McGrew (1992b). It is not absolutely necessary to demonstrate that the nation-state is in decline in order to support a case for political globalization. Indeed, the emergence of the nation-state is itself a product of globalization processes. As is discussed in Chapter 3, Giddens shows that the institutionalization of the nation-state occurred within the context of an elaborating system of international relations that began in the nineteenth century. Nations could only survive and operate within that system if they had a centralized and unified governmental system that could steer their affairs and manage their security. The demise of the feudally based and absolutist continental empires of Tsarist Russia and Austria-Hungary and the later dismantling of the European colonial empires bear witness to the success of the nation-state in blending citizen commitment with administrative effectiveness and international security. We begin then with developments at the level of the state.

THE CRISIS OF THE STATE

The development of the modern state can be understood to have occurred in two historical phases. In caricature, the first or liberal phase covers the nineteenth century while the second or organized phase covers the twentieth (see Crook *et al*. 1992: 79–105; Lash and Urry 1987). The transformation of feudal monarchies originally took two directions. In the first, found in Russia and continental Europe, the powers of the feudal nobility were progressively centralized in the hands of absolute monarchs. By contrast with this maximal concentration of political power, a more important development was the emergence of a minimal or liberal state in England, Holland and the USA. Here political power could be shared democratically because the state enjoyed little sovereignty. Its role was principally external, using military force and diplomacy to secure raw materials, foreign trade and immigrant labour. Its internal role was restricted to effecting dispute resolution by instituting a regime of law, protecting private property and maintaining order in the industrial labour force. The struggle for political domination took place beyond the confines of the state within the relationship between capitalists and workers.

The twentieth-century organized state represents a combination of the centralization of absolutism with the administrative efficiency of the liberal state. Its development is associated with the world wars, the great depression, and the communist and fascist revolutions that accompanied them. The liberal state was inadequate to deal with these globalized fractures and stresses, particularly insofar as it was unable to mobilize the commitments of diverse interest groups in the solution of national problems. It was therefore reorganized on a corporatist basis to deal with threats not only to national security but to national economic welfare. The state became focused on an executive core that now engaged in two principal practices. First, it became much more interventionary in providing central planning and economic and fiscal management in particular. Second, it acted as an intermediary between societal interest groups, especially between employers and employees. Its main strategies were to support investment and industrial development with a view to expanding domestic economic activity. The fascist and communist examples often cultivated popular support for such activity by adopting an expansive and aggressive international posture but in the second half of the century most organized states signed up for military bloc alliance systems with a view to safeguarding their own socio-political systems.

A key feature of these corporatist states was the cultivation of mass support. In the democratic examples an obvious mechanism was the franchise but even the communist states operated a version of popular democracy through the party. In order to maintain this support and in order to control interest-articulation by employees, states moved in the direction of welfarism. The material benefits of economic expansion and international stability were thus not to be confined to capitalists but to be redistributed across the population. The redistributive mechanisms included a progressive system of income taxation, a 'safety net' for the financially distressed, generalized health, education and pension schemes, and often state acquisition of key industries. By the middle of the twentieth century most states, including the new ex-colonial ones, had adopted a variant of welfare corporatism that included many or all of these measures.

In the third quarter of the twentieth century the corporate welfare state hit a multiple and widely recognized crisis. Its components were as follows (Crook *et al.* 1992: 92–7).

- Popular demands escalated beyond the capacity of the state to meet them. The right to make a claim against the state had been separated from the capacity to make an economic contribution to it. Moreover the state had educated and politically enfranchised its population. The volume and effectiveness of collective claims against the state was clogging the political process.

- The locations of real state power became hidden. Politicians focused on mediating claims and cultivating support while the real power was exercised behind the scenes by bureaucrats and technicians.
- The administration of welfare was consuming an increasing proportion of the welfare budget. Moreover the welfare system was cultivating its own clients by creating a culture of state dependency.
- The interventions of the state in economic matters tended to destabilize the markets which they were intended to preserve. Economies were populated by weak and failing industries and under-employed workers.
- The class-interest groups on which the corporatist state had been founded were decomposing in favour of new status groups, often with 'postmaterialist' value-commitments that the materialist strategies of corporatism could not meet.
- The state could no longer offer security: trade and financial markets were internationalized; drug syndicates and terrorists no longer respected borders; the 'natural' issues of AIDS and ecology were not susceptible to state action; and the individual state was no protection against the risks of chemical and nuclear weapons.
- Lastly, through international alliances, the state was creating more danger than security. It divided the world into hostile camps whose commitments to the acquisition of military technology could only have one purpose.

The response to this multiple crisis was a process of disétatization or state-weakening. The corporate interest groups that previously had supported the state began to downscale and localize. Trade unions shrunk and were displaced by local interest groups and civic initiatives. State intervention by command was reduced but at the same time states sought to increase the scope and scale of the market. Many government services were opened to competitive tendering between the public and private sectors and, as is well known, many state-owned industries were returned to the private sector. Many states stopped providing welfare in certain areas and others moved towards demilitarization. They also partially surrendered their sovereignty by participating in global and regional organizations.

The implications of the crisis of the state and consequent disétatization for globalization have both obvious and less obvious aspects. Clearly any breakdown in the nation-state system leaves an opening for political globalization. So long as the state persists, a sovereign world polity is impossible. The less obvious aspects might be more important, however. The crisis of the state contributes to the reflexivity of globalization. This is because the excuses of politicians for their failures have taken on a global hue: our economy is failing because of the recession in the USA or Europe or Japan or somewhere else; our currency is declining because of the activities of unidentified international speculators; our air is dirty because someone else has had a nuclear meltdown; we cannot solve the problem of urban crime because it is fed by international drugs syndicates; or, we cannot feed our people because the level of international aid is not adequate. Insofar as politicians deflect blame on to the global arena, collective political actors will focus their attention on that arena and the nation-state will progressively become an irrelevance. We can now consider the globalized political issues on which they are focusing and their effects on the sovereignty of the state.

PLANETARY PROBLEMS

One of the key features of the system of international relations set up by the new nation-states of the nineteenth century was the principle of sovereignty. This principle asserts that the state has the absolute right to determine autonomously the internal fate of the nation for which it constitutes the set of political arrangements. Under this principle, interference by one state in the internal affairs of another is regarded as pathological.[1] Under current globalized circumstances this principle is frequently breached on a multilateral basis on the grounds that the inhabitants of the planet experience a set of common problems that can be exacerbated by the actions of an individual nation-state. This development represents, at the minimum, a 'nationalization' of global issues, an expectation that national policies must address the common problems of the planet.

Human rights

Perhaps the key development is the institutionalization of the view that individual human beings have rights *qua* humans that can be sustained against the sovereignty of the state. Historically rights have been understood as an étatocentric issue. They were institutionalized in citizenship and they grew as the state developed from its liberal form through corporatism and welfarism. Although widely contested, Marshall's view (1973) that citizenship rights expand from the legal (*habeas corpus*, etc.) to the political (e.g. the franchise) to the economic (a minimum material standard of living) offers much as a paradigmatic state-ment of this development. Within this view citizenship is con-ceived as an expanding set of obligations maintained by the state towards its subjects that also involves a progressive limitation of its sovereignty over them.

A crucial event that undermined state sovereignty in these terms was the Nuremburg trials of Nazi 'war criminals' prosecuted by the victorious powers after the Second World War. Here 'fol-lowing orders' given by the German state proved to be no defence against an accusation of crimes against humanity. Indeed the judicial tribunal went so far as to specify that, where state laws are in conflict with international norms specifying human rights, individuals must exercise a 'moral choice' and transgress the state laws (Held 1991: 220). However, moral choice has in subsequent prosecutions not proved to be a successful defence – claims by traitors that they are undermining the security of the state in order to protect humanity, and by draft dodgers that they are conscientious objectors have proved notably unsuccessful.

There have been frequent declarations of universal human rights, normally involving freedom of speech and action, freedom of political association and participation, due process under law, minimum access to health, education and material welfare, and control of one's own body, especially its reproductive capacities. However, states frequently violate these principles because the conventions offer no means of collective enforcement. A notable exception is the European Convention for the Protection of Human Rights and Freedoms (1950) that allows individuals to petition the European Commission on Human Rights, which may ask the European Court of Human Rights to enforce the relevant UN convention (Held 1991: 219). A far more important aspect of the internationalization of human rights is their political rather than legal enforcement. Extreme and public violations of human rights often meet with widespread global condemnation and frequently with multilateral political action. Among the more notable examples we can mention the patchy though effective economic, sporting and cultural sanctions against the white racist regimes of Rhodesia (Zimbabwe) and then South Africa, the diplomatic and economic isolation of China following the Tiananmen Square suppression of political freedoms in 1988, and the UN interventions in Bosnia and Somalia that began in 1992 in order to protect civilian populations from war-induced threats of starvation and violence. 'Human rights' has thus become an important legitimizing icon that can allow interventions by one or more states in the internal affairs of others with relatively widespread global support.

The planetary environment

The above discussion of human rights can confirm the point made in Chapter 3 that one of the most important aspects of globalization is that it connects the local with the general. Human rights connect the individual with humanity by asserting that each individual is an instance of humanity. Another 'planetary problem' achieves this just as effectively – the issue of environmentalism that connects subjective lifestyles with the physical condition of the planet. Many inhabitants of the planet, especially those fortunate enough to be affluent, are beginning to see the earth as a common home that needs to be maintained and tended if they and their individual descendants are to have a comfortable, prosperous and healthy life. A particularly globalizing aspect of this conceptualization is the view that human society cannot infinitely be expanded beyond the physical limits of the earth and its constituent resources. The environmentalist architect Buckminster Fuller's 1980s characterization of the planet as 'spaceship earth' neatly conveys the notion that it is bounded in space.

Perhaps the first popularized attempt to specify these limits was the report of the Club of Rome, a group of concerned public intellectuals (Meadows *et al.* 1976). The report pointed out that both population and economic growth are limited by the capacity of the planet to accommodate them. The limits are threefold: food, mineral and energy resources, and pollution. The Club's Malthusian arguments about them were as follows:

- Food production is based on the availability of arable land. Even if the productivity of arable land were doubled, because the supply of arable land is falling, the world population will be unable to be fed at some point prior to 2050 AD. In some parts of the world that point has already arrived.
- The crisis is even more severe with respect to non-renewable resources of minerals and energy.
- A rapidly increasing population with an increasing economic growth rate also produces pollutants – heat, carbon dioxide, nuclear waste, and chemical waste, which can seriously impede its own capacity to survive. The rate of outputs of pollutants is increasing exponentially along with population size and economic growth.

On these arguments the world finds itself in what may be called a population-resources trap in which a feedback system operates to exacerbate an already problematic situation. The more population increases, the more it uses up non-renewable resources and increases pollution. Resource shortages and pollution costs reduce international capacity to engage in sustained long-term economic growth. Yet economic growth is the engine which modernizes societies and alters traditional values about family size and age of marriage and thus has a constraining effect on fertility. If these traditional orientations do not change then population will continue to increase and the cycle will begin again.

The issues identified by the Club of Rome, problems of starvation, resource depletion and pollution, remain salient. More recently public attention has focused on two specific areas in which these problems are having a particular and pressing effect: biodiversity and global warming. So pressing have they become that they were the central topics at the first Earth Summit intergovernmental conference in Rio de Janeiro in 1992.

Biodiversity is the issue of the maintenance of multiple species of plants and animals on the planet. There are two threats to biodiversity. The most obvious is economic exploitation – this has led to the depletion of such publicly prominent species as the rhinoceros, the African elephant and the great whales. The second and more significant threat comes from the destruction of habitat. As human populations expand they extend urban environments, extend agricultural activity, and expand their exploitation of natural resources of minerals and timber, thus destroying natural habitat. As they migrate, humans carry with them exotic species and introduce them to new environments. All these activities can upset delicately balanced ecosystems in such a way as to make it impossible for many indigenous species to survive. Such activity is responsible for the probable extinction of the Tasmanian tiger (Thylacine) and other species currently threatened include the Kouprey (10 left), the Javan rhinoceros (50), the Iriomote cat (60), the black lion tamarin (130) and the pygmy hog (150) (*Melbourne Sunday Age* 31/5/92).

Global warming is a catch-all phrase which covers four developments: depletion of the ozone layer; atmospheric pollution; deforestation; and climatic change.

- The ozone layer is a high-level stratum of the atmosphere which screens the surface of the planet from intense ultra-violet radiation. It was discovered to be thinning over Antarctica in the mid–1980s and by 1991 had suffered a depletion of 3 per cent in temperate regions (*Economist* 30/5/92). It is of particular concern to human beings because high levels of ultra-violet radiation are associated with high levels of skin cancer. The main cause of depletion of the ozone layer is the emission of the inert gases called chloro-fluoro carbons (CFCs) used as propellents in aerosol sprays and in refrigeration systems. An international protocol signed in Montreal in 1987 has effectively reduced CFC emissions but it is unclear whether the ozone layer will recover and how long it will take to do so.
- Scientists have long been aware of the effects of both hydrocarbon emissions from cars and industrial sulphur dioxide pollution which returns as acid rain to destroy forests. A more recent concern has been industrial emissions of carbon dioxide from the burning of fossil fuel. The level of such emissions is associated with the level of industrial development of a society. The USA emits about 5.5 tonnes per head per year for example, while Brazil emits less than one tonne per head (*Economist* 30/5/92). Carbon dioxide and methane (produced by pastoral production) are 'greenhouse gases' – they prevent reverse radiation of solar heat thus raising the temperature of the planet.
- The effects of greenhouse gases are exacerbated by

progressive deforestation in the wet tropics. Trees extract carbon from the atmosphere, trap it, and emit separated oxygen. Deforestation reduces the amount of carbon dioxide taken up and also releases previously trapped carbon by burning. Since 1850 about 7.7 million square kilometres of forest (about 12 per cent of the total, or an area the size of the USA) have disappeared (*Melbourne Sunday Age* 31/5/92).

- Many scientists agree that the above developments will lead to a raising of the temperature of the planet. However, there is widespread disagreement about the extent and speed of the warming process and about its effects on different areas. The most recent United Nations estimate suggests that the surface temperature will rise between 2 and 4.5 degrees in the next century (*Melbourne Sunday Age* 31/5/92). The consequences may well be serious for food production and sea levels.

Public consciousness of these problems has been raised by a series of popular scientific publications that seek to raise the alarm. The first Club of Rome report is an early example but consciousness of planetary problems has come a long way since then. Perhaps the most extreme statement of the earth as a single entity is Lovelock's 'Gaia hypothesis' (named after the Greek goddess of the earth) which proposed that:

the entire range of living matter on Earth, from whales to viruses, and from oaks to algae, could be regarded as constituting a single living entity, capable of manipulating the Earth's atmosphere to suit its overall needs and endowed with faculties and powers far beyond those of its constituent parts.

(Lovelock 1987: 9)

This stunning piece of gynomorphism was embellished by the claim that if Gaia was threatened by human action she would turn on human beings and eliminate them. If believed, this argument would be alarming enough but at least Gaia is a predictable system. By contrast 'chaos theory' (Gleich 1987; Hall 1992a) asserts that global and other systems are interconnected but inherently disorderly. As they evolve, minute perturbations can amplify very rapidly. The condition of the planet is not only full of danger but this danger can be exacerbated rapidly by inadvertent individual events, perhaps a single nuclear melt-down or oil-spill. An environmentalist (and sociological) version of chaos theory can be found in Beck's analysis of the emerging 'risk society', which he argues to be fraught with unpredictable dangers (1992; see Chapter 3). Like Lovelock and Gleich, Beck has found immense publishing success by contributing to the global environmental panic.[2]

O'Neill indicates that such panics are both the product of and contributors to globalization:

> By a *globalizing panic* I understand any practice that traverses the world to reduce the world and its cultural diversity to the generics of coca-cola, tourism, foreign aid, medical aid, military defence posts, tourism, fashion, and the international money-markets. Since these practices are never quite stabilized, their dynamics include deglobalizing tendencies which will be reinscribed by the global system as threats to the 'world order'.
>
> (O'Neill 1992: 332)

O'Neill's example of a globalizing panic is AIDS, which might itself be considered an 'environmental' threat in the technical sense that the organic body is part of the physical environment of the social.[3] Such panics undermine the legitimacy of problem-solving states not only because they do not respect territorial boundaries but because they are in principle insoluble by any state. They disempower state establishments.

The political leaders of nation-states have responded to the fears of their panicked constituencies in the only way possible, that is by reducing the sovereignty of their states relative to international arrangements. Notable examples include the nuclear test ban and non-proliferation treaties, the various conventions on the law of the sea signed between 1967 and 1982, and the Vienna Convention of 1985 and Montreal Protocol of 1987 in which national governments agreed to limit emissions of CFCs and carbon monoxide. In so doing certain sectors of the planetary environment have been relocated outside the territorial sovereignty of nation-states – they have been redefined as 'global commons' (Vogler 1992). They include, to varying degrees and with varying levels of enforcement, the high seas, the seabed, fisheries, marine mammals, satellite orbits, the moon, the airwaves, the atmosphere, and the entire continent of Antarctica. These commons once established require management on an international scale if they are to be conserved against the prospect of unlimited economic exploitation.

Development and inequality

The previous chapter specifies some of the details of the way in which the core of the world's economy is managed on an international scale – financial markets were originally managed through the IMF although they are now decentralized, trade is managed through WTO (formerly GATT), and economic policy coordination through G7. However, none of these coordinating agencies gives attention to what might be viewed as the central problem of the global political economy, that of gross differences in income and wealth between its constituent sub-economies and the relations of domination and subordination that arise between them. As the preceding chapter shows, the increasing integration of rich with poor sub-economies is tending to stabilize a class system at the global level. In previous eras international relationships of inequality were viewed as the non-problematic outcome of the superiority of the dominating race or society. In current circumstances they are often viewed as morally repugnant but more frequently as problematic in terms of their capacity to disrupt the global economy as a whole.

The first evidence that global inequality was viewed as a common political problem was the institutionalization of economic aid programmes established individually by most of the capitalist rich societies in the 1950s and 1960s. Aid programmes typically had one of three ostensive objectives: to 'band-aid' specific threats to human life and welfare such as temporary famine; to prime the local economic pump by financing such strategic projects as dams and steel mills; or to break down social or cultural barriers to development including the introduction of birth-control programmes. Financial transfers were often accompanied by teams of technical experts and volunteer aid workers, of whom the US Peace Corps is the best known example. Such development aid was only infrequently altruistic or recipient controlled: it was often directed to ex-colonies or established spheres of influence; it was often linked with military aid as a way of maintaining a particular ideological cast on the host state; and it frequently insisted that aid monies be spent in purchasing items from the donor society. Almost everywhere, the donors had a clear commitment to maintaining markets for manufactured goods and stable, low-cost supplies of raw materials in the host societies.

Aid formed part of a spectrum of relationships, including trade and debt, between rich and poor states that appeared to reinforce global inequality. By the 1970s the development issue centred a crisis of legitimation in these relationships – claims to morality in the way in which rich states treated poor ones could no longer be sustained. Two social scientific theories effectively delegitimized the relationship (Gilpin 1987: 274–88). The first is the so-called Singer-Prebisch or structuralist argument. This suggests that rich states have dynamic economies committed to technological advancement in which monopoly corporations and effective labour unions can hold up the prices of manufactured goods. Meanwhile poor states have feeble investment patterns and a disorganized labour force, which means that there is constant downward pressure on commodity prices and no incentive to industrial diversification. This produces a consistent tendency towards increasing disparity between the prices of manufactured goods and raw materials that makes development impossible. By contrast, dependency theory, as we saw in Chapter 2, concentrates on the allocation of capital. International capitalists, it is argued, deliberately use capital allocation to control the pattern of development in LDCs, and indeed they argue that capitalism in the MDCs could not flourish unless there was a deliberate suppression of indigenous development.

These arguments led to the UNCTAD-sponsored conference of 1974, of which Prebisch was the general secretary, and which established the NIEO discussed in the previous chapter. Here all states agreed in principle to improve aid, redress the growing disparity in the terms of trade, and give LDCs more power within the organs of global economic management. In fact, however, few of these goals have come to be realized and, as we have seen, the international economic order in general has become more disorderly and decentralized.

Peace and order

By 1945 the international system had suffered the depradations of two world wars and of consequent revolutions and economic upheavals. The system of competing sovereign states, able to use force at will, established by the Treaty of Westphalia of 1648, that had ensured peace for much of the nineteenth century, had now clearly failed. Moreover technological developments in the area of nuclear weapons and their delivery systems meant that any further outbreak of global war represented a genuine threat to the survival of life as a whole. The world was no longer safe for capitalism or any other system of social power.

In 1945 fifty-one nations, mainly the victors in that war, met in San Francisco and set up a new system that sought to constrain violence between states on the basis of a set of enforceable norms. The principles of that United Nations charter to which they agreed were as follows (Cassese 1991: 263):

- war and the use of force between states was prohibited;
- a monopoly on the use of force was vested in the Security Council of the United Nations Organization which was expected to use military means to maintain collective security and to constrain aggression; and
- states could only use force to defend themselves against aggression by another state.

Clearly the UN has never managed to enforce collective security other than in two doubtful cases: the 'defence' of South Korea against aggression from North Korea and its Chinese ally in the early 1950s; and the 'defence' of Kuwait against invasion from Iraq in 1988. In these doubtful cases the UN acted as a legitimizing umbrella for direct action by the USA and its allies. Otherwise it has engaged in 'peace-keeping' operations which merely serve to keep the protagonists apart. It has failed to prevent protracted wars in Israel/Palestine, Afghanistan and, most notably, Vietnam, as well as numerous minor conflagrations.

Nevertheless the UN system represents a very clear advance on the Westphalian system and is clear evidence that peace and security is a shared global problem that can neither be left to private treaties between states nor to the dubious intentions of any hegemon. Moreover the existence of the UN has established a communicative and normative framework for clearly positive developments in the control of the most destructive means of violence. These include the nuclear test ban treaty of 1961, the nuclear non-proliferation treaty of 1968, the various strategic arms reduction agreements of the 1970s and 1980s, and the Helsinki Accord that set up The European Council for Security and Co-operation (ECSC).

The redefinition of social problems as global problems under-mines the sovereignty of the state in three ways:

- it redirects individual political preferences;
- it delegitimizes the nation-state as a problem-solver;
- it sets up new international organizations to which some elements of state sovereignty are progressively sur-rendered.[4]

We can now examine these emerging global organizations.

INTERNATIONAL ORGANIZATIONS

In this section we examine the extent to which planetary society has moved in the direction of a globalized polity. To speak of a globalized polity can invoke the image of a world government, a single unitary and centralized state similar to contemporary nation-states, or even a world empire. This need not be the case. A globalized polity can have the characteristics of a network of power centres, including nation-states, coordinated by means other than command. In principle such power centres might be coordinated because their controllers shared common norms and common interests and sought to move towards consensus on such issues. Such a view is not as romantically optimistic as it may appear. Regional groupings of states, such as the EU, and a wide range of specialized interest associations already coordinate their activities on just such a basis. However such an outcome is less likely than a polity organized as a market, or more precisely as multiple markets. Here processes of allocation (e.g. of welfare, economic development, peace and security, pollution, cultural performances) would be governed by competition between power centres much in the way that global flows of finance or of infor-mation are the consequences of multiple and complex decisions.

The vehicles within which these parallel processes of consensus building and competition can occur are international organizations. Political scientists normally make a distinction between two types of international organization: inter-govern-mental organizations (IGOs) and international non-governmental organizations (INGOs). Individually such organizations are not necessarily global in scope and indeed may cover as few as two national societies. However, taken together they constitute a web-like global network through which goal setting and allocative

decisions can flow. IGOs include not only the obvious organizations of whole states, such as the UN or ITU, but also links
between the parts of governmental systems, between parliaments,
central banks or environmental departments. Such links are greatest in the areas defined as common global problems. INGOs
might be regarded as more important in globalization terms than
IGOs because they outflank nation-states and threaten borders.
They are unruly because their complexity defies command and
their capacity to link diverse people in relation to common causes
and interests undermines the saliency of the state.

Many date the initial development of international organizations at around 1920 (e.g. Archer 1983: 3; Giddens 1985: 261–2).
Prior to that date international relations had been conducted
largely by means of the state-based systems of trade, diplomacy,
colonialism, military alliance and war. Only in the areas of postal
communications and health regulation was there serious previous
IGO activity. A critical turning point was the Versailles peace
conference which sought to impose an international order in the
aftermath of the First World War. It took two critical measures:
it gave states to the nationalities of the dismembered Austro-
Hungarian, Ottoman, Prussian and Russian empires; and it set
up a League of Nations to serve as an umbrella for the thirty or
so IGOs that already existed and to act as a forum for consensus
building on issues of peace and security. However, the League was
to fail because the USA turned isolationist and, having originally
promoted the idea, refused to join, because the Fascist and Communist states were not members, and because the organization
had no power of enforcement at its disposal. It collapsed with
the outbreak of the Second World War in 1939.

The close of that war in 1945 marked the emergence of a far
more effective IGO system. The key developments were the
establishment of the UN (discussed in the preceding section) and
its subordinate agencies FAO, UNCTAD, UNESCO, UNICEF,
UNRRA, WHO, the IMF, World Bank, and GATT (see Chapter
4), and the military alliance systems, CENTO, NATO, SEATO
and the Warsaw Treaty Organization (see below). More recent
developments include IGOs for regional economic cooperation
and trade and for monitoring environmental degradation and
population control. There has therefore been a marked upswing
in the number of IGOs since 1945 and in 1992 they numbered
over 3,000 (UIA 1992: 1671).

The burgeoning growth of INGOs has been even more

remarkable. Some examples given by McGrew (1992b: 8) can illustrate their importance and the breadth of their activities. They include environmental pressure groups (e.g. Friends of the Earth, Greenpeace, WWF); professional and academic associations (e.g. Association of Commonwealth Universities, International Sociological Association); religious forums (e.g. World Council of Churches, World Moslem Congress); sports organizations (e.g. International Olympic Committee, International Cricket Conference); and welfare organizations (e.g. International Federation of Red Cross and Red Crescent Societies, Caritas). By 1992 there were nearly 15,000 such organizations, excluding MNCs and BINGOs (Business INGOs). Together they constitute a complex and ungovernable web of relationships that extends beyond the nation-state.

An examination of the growth pattern of states, IGOs and INGOs can confirm the pattern of periodicity in the globalization process that is discussed throughout this book. As Figure 5.1 shows, the international system was, until the First World War, numerically dominated by states and their mainly bilateral relations. IGOs were very few in number and INGOs almost non-existent. An expansion of the global system began in the first quarter of the twentieth century when all three types of organization grew rapidly in number and importance. However, in the second half of the twentieth century the world was dominated by IGOs in which states surrendered a considerable measure of their sovereignty. A key feature of the accelerated phase of globalization since about 1960 has been the rapid growth of INGOs which lends support to the claim that the main thrust of this phase is cultural, rather than material or political, in character.[5] The question of how much power the INGOs actually have will obviously be a major point of debate but their existence and expansion should at least convince us that their value and effectiveness is in little doubt for those individuals who construct them. It is also clear that national governments are obliged to take IGOs and INGOs seriously and treat with them.

THREE WORLDS INTO ONE

In the 1970s a cult of strategic gaming spread through the university campuses of North America. Two games, 'Diplomacy' and the more ominously named 'Risk' became commercially popular.

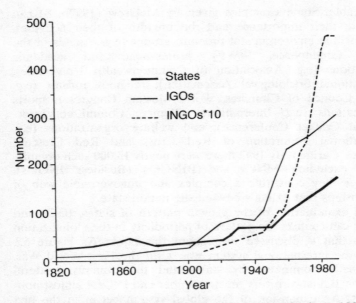

Figure 5.1 Growth of states and international organizations, 1820–1990
Data sources: Giddens 1985: 264; McGrew 1992b: 8, 12

In these games the participants would role play nation-states and would act without morality or loyalty in furthering their interests, occasionally to the extent of subjective personal conflict. International relations in the nineteenth century operated much as these games did. Britain, for example could fight against France in the Napoleonic War, then with France forty years later in the Crimea, and stay neutral during the Franco-Prussian War of the 1870s. There were no stable blocs or alliances and even the Triple Alliance (Germany, Austria-Hungary, Italy) and the Triple Entente (Britain, France, Russia) that emerged at the end of that century were temporary and hasty marriages intended conveniently to manage specific problems.

The peace treaties that closed the First World War did little to move international relations in a truly global direction but rather confirmed its fragmentation. France and Britain sought to reassert a faltering international leadership; America isolated itself; Germany was plundered and excluded; and Russia was a pariah state. For all Western intents and purposes the rest of the world, including China and Japan, did not exist. Throughout that period international relations were without a world focus. States sought to manage their interests in terms of bilateral relations with other states rather than seeking to establish a global system in which these interests might prosper.

The Second World War changed this view by making it very clear: first, that global conflict threatened every nation-state whether it chose to be involved or not (*vide* Pearl Harbour); second, that only the collective security of stable alliances could protect states from aggression; third, that to exclude or to beggar other nation-states would often lead to instability. The Yalta and Potsdam conferences that occurred between the three main victorious powers (Britain, USA, USSR) at the end of that war intentionally constructed a global system of international relations by explicitly dividing the world into spheres of influence and assigning them to the victors: Eastern and Central Europe to the Soviet Union; Western Europe to Britain, France and the USA; the Middle East, Africa, South and South-East Asia to Britain and France; the Asia-Pacific region and Latin America to the USA. Eventually Britain and France proved to be too weak, economically and militarily, to sustain global influence and their spheres passed to the USA.

Thus the world became divided between two superpowers that dominated it by three means. First, they armed themselves to the teeth with nuclear weapons, long-range delivery systems and rapid deployment forces, which enabled them to give their power a global reach and to place each other in a situation of mutual threat. Second, they established alliance systems in their spheres of interest that established protective buffer regions that could absorb aggression and aggregated national armed forces. The Soviet dominated system, the Warsaw Treaty Organization, included its 'satellite' states in Eastern Europe, while the USA dominated NATO, the Western European alliance, SEATO in South-East Asia, and CENTO a central Asian alliance inherited from Britain. Third, they intervened and competed in areas where their influence was in dispute, that is in parts of Asia, Africa and Latin America. Often that intervention involved direct military aggression, as in the US invasions of Korea and Vietnam and the Soviet invasion of Afghanistan, but more frequently it took the form of advice, aid, military assistance to sympathetic regimes as well as covert operations.

By these means the globe was divided into two worlds, East

and West. The superpower system was, for the most part, stable.
The superpowers agreed to respect each other's sphere of influence. When Soviet forces moved to repress anti-state forces in
Hungary in 1957 and in Czechoslovakia in 1968, for example, the
West merely expressed horror and took no action. This commitment was reinforced by the knowledge that any pre-emptive
nuclear strike on the opponent would not destroy its military
capability sufficiently to render the aggressor immune – to destroy
the opponent would be to destroy the planet. So convincing was
this imperative that for much of this so-called 'cold war' period
the superpowers practised a form of diplomacy known as
'détente' in which they sought to establish bilateral norms for
their competition.

As is indicated above that competition remained at its most
intense in what became known as the 'third world', the ex-colonial
states of Africa, Asia and Latin America. These sought to establish themselves as an alternative and neutral source of global
influence. Being impoverished, their only leverage came from
their ability to play one superpower off against the other. This
meant that each individual state tended at least to 'tilt' towards
either the USA or the USSR and the third-world movement was
seldom cohesive. Nevertheless many nations managed to maintain
a moderately independent foreign policy.

Under contemporary conditions the three-world or superpower system is hyperdifferentiating. We can no longer identify
three worlds or two superpowers but rather a singular system in
which the critical basis for international relations is no longer the
ownership of military hardware but both economic muscle and
the ability to influence ideas and commitments. The sources of
these changes are the following:

- The Soviet system proved unable to provide its citizens
  with a standard of living similar to that found in the West
  while simultaneously maintaining a command economy
  and a globally active military force. In 1989 the USSR gave
  up its attempt to control Eastern Europe where market
  democracies rapidly emerged. The USSR itself then demo-
  cratized and defederated and Russia can no longer be
  regarded unambiguously as a superpower. Many ex-satel-
  lites and ex-Soviet republics are now seeking NATO and
  EU membership.
- The USA is unable to maintain its influence in Europe

and the Far East, given its economic decline. American industry is wilting in the face of global competition and throughout the 1980s the military budget could only be sustained by high levels of deficit financing.

- New power centres have emerged in Japan and the EU. This power was originally economic in character but is now extending to diplomatic and military arenas.
- Third-world states are experiencing rapid economic differentiation so that they no longer constitute a homogeneous community of the disadvantaged. This differentiation began with the development of OPEC (see Chapter 4) which ensured the escalation of the GDPs of oil-producing states. More recently, the rapid industrialization of the NICs has placed them closer in their interests and commitments to the first world than to the third.

A specific outcome of these developments has been the merging of military actions undertaken on behalf of such defence alliances as NATO with peacekeeping operations carried out on behalf of the UN. The most important instance was the intervention of an American-headed expeditionary force that recovered the state of Kuwait following an Iraqi invasion in 1988. While the force was clearly an alliance of Western capitalist with traditional Middle Eastern interests it operated under UN auspices and with the sanction of the Security Council. Equally it is unclear whether the European peacekeeping troops operating in the former Yugoslavia in the early 1990s were acting on behalf of the UN, NATO or the EU. Certainly, such developments indicate that in many instances national interests are becoming merged into global ones.

There are three possible theoretical interpretations of these developments. The first suggests the emergence of a 'new world order', a liberal construct that implies the disappearance of the superpowers and the emergence of a highly differentiated yet relatively consensual family of nations that punishes the deviant and protects the defenceless. This is clearly an ideological conception that seeks to obscure very real differences of interest and military power. The second is the suggestion that the USA won the cold war and that the world is dominated by an unchallenged hegemon. Curiously this view appears to be the property both of leftist critics and rightist triumphalists. It fails in the light of American impotence in Vietnam, Iran and Somalia. The USA succeeded in Kuwait but only with allied military support, UN legitimacy, tacit Russian acceptance, and European, Japanese and Arab financial assistance. This suggests that a third interpretation, that of the emergence of a multipolar world, has much to offer as a realistic assessment. The domination of the superpowers has disappeared to be replaced by a fluid and highly differentiated pattern of international relations that exhibits much of the chaos and uncertainty that is also found, for example, in financial markets.

A specific outcome that can confirm the arrival of this newly disordered world is the way in which the territoriality and sovereignty of states is being reinterpreted. The ex-Soviet republics are universally recognized as states yet they have extremely porous borders and precious little substantive independence. The key point of pressure here is the issue of nationality – the Baltic states, for example, cannot remain entirely separate from Russia so long as they include substantial Russian minorities. National pressure has been felt in a different way in ex-Yugoslavia and ex-Czechoslovakia leading to their dissolution into almost borderless nationalities. This development is paralleled in a spectacular way by the formation of the EU and to a lesser extent by NAFTA. The former is seeking to remove customs barriers and inspections and passport controls as well as seeking to aggregate such state norms as citizenship rights at a continental level. Equally its constituent nation-states are experiencing a resurgence of minority nationalisms in such diverse locations as Scotland, Flanders, Catalonia and Lombardy. In general the firmness of the linkage, state-societal community-nation-territory, that had been imposed by the realpolitik of the superpower order, is widely being called into question.

A NEW POLITICAL CULTURE

The possibility of a borderless world is enhanced to the extent that there is a common political culture across societies. To the extent that governments share ideological commitments and interests they will be more prepared to see aggregation or decentralization of state sovereignty and also to dismantle protective and defensive barriers between one another.

The case for the emergence of a single political culture is made most strongly by Fukuyama (1992) and Huntington (1991). We need not concern ourselves here with Fukuyama's theoretical explanation, which is a version of Hegelian essentialism that asserts that the human desire for individual 'recognition' drives a universal history in the direction of such a singularity. Rather we can concentrate on the empirical case that he sets out. His argument, like Huntington's, is that the national societies of the world have moved or are moving towards a political culture of liberal democracy. The central ideas of such a culture are: first that individuals should have rights to autonomy in certain spheres of thought and action including, for example, due process under law, speech and publication that expresses political or religious ideas, control of the body, and ownership and disposal of property; and second that the members of any polity should have the right to choose and to participate in their own government by means which roughly give them an equal influence in that choice and an equal chance to participate (Fukuyama 1992: 42–3). Contentiously, he is quite clear that liberal democracy implies a commitment to market capitalism because these guarantee individual rights in the economic sphere. He also stresses that it is the culture rather than practice of liberal democracy that is critical. In triumphalist tone, he asserts: 'What is emerging victorious ... is not so much liberal practice, as the liberal *idea*. That is to say, for a very large part of the world, there is now no ideology with pretensions to universality that is in a position to challenge liberal democracy' (1992: 45, original italics).[6]

The global predominance of liberal democracy was accomplished in a series of waves punctuated by fallbacks that began with liberal revolutions in Europe and America in the seventeenth and eighteenth centuries. However, the main developments occurred within what we have come to recognize as the accelerated phase of globalization, the last third of the twentieth century. In this period authoritarian regimes, first of the right and then of the left, began to collapse. In the 1970s fascist or military dictatorships folded in Spain, Portugal, Greece and Turkey. In the 1980s liberal democracies were established in the former dictatorships of Latin America; Korea, the Philippines, Taiwan, and Thailand also moved in that direction; and there is now the very real prospect that the culture will take root in South Africa as well as in other parts of that continent. Fukuyama argues that the dictatorial regimes in these states were toppled by a crisis of legitimacy, their governments were no longer seen as representing society as a whole. The collapse or weakening of state socialist regimes in the 1980s and 1990s was even more dramatic. Here both Fukuyama and Huntington give weight to the inability to deliver economic prosperity without the liberal institutions of capitalism but equally stress the issue of the legitimacy of authoritarian regimes in the face of prevailing global democratic norms (see especially Huntington 1991: 106).

The outcome of these developments is shown in Figure 5.2 which gives the number of liberal-democratic states in the global system. This number doubled between 1975 and 1991 so that about 60 of the world's large societies are now liberal democracies. The main exceptions are the remaining socialist states of East Asia and Islamic theocracies, monarchies and military dictatorships. Many of the latter also display some of the characteristics of liberal democracy – Iran, for example, is democratic in that it has relatively free and fair elections but not liberal in that the citizen is without rights; China is clearly undemocratic but is liberalizing in the economic sphere; equally, democratic practices in Singapore and Hong Kong have been questioned in some quarters but their liberality is unchallenged. Nor do the data include the effects of recent developments in ex-Yugoslavia, the ex-USSR, or South Africa.

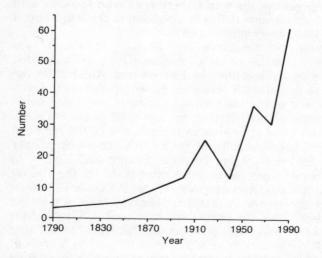

Figure 5.2 Liberal democratic states, 1790–1990: estimates by Fukuyama and Huntington
Data source: Fukuyama 1992: 49–50

However we must also consider the possibility of cultural variation between liberal democracies – for example in Sweden a high level of state intervention and personal taxation has historically been more positively valued than in the USA which tends to value personal autonomy above equality of condition. Here too there is evidence of cultural convergenge. A shift is under way towards a culture described by Inglehart (1990) as the rise of post-materialist values. The traditional focus of politics in liberal democracies was material values, issues to do with the distribution and redistribution of goods and services. The typical division in this politics was between a 'right' or conservative side that stressed the preservation of property ownership and freedom of contract in markets, often coupled with a paternalistic welfarism, and a 'left' or social democratic side that stressed the redistribution of property and income on a more egalitarian basis, a state-interventionist welfare system and the regulation of markets. Post-materialist values emphasize community, self-expression and the quality of life. Here a political value division emerges between a 'new right' which stresses individual autonomy, the right to consume and governmental minimalism and a 'new left' that stresses the empowerment of minorities and a mutuality of interests among human beings and between them and their environments. Inglehart estimates that by 1970 post-materialists outnumbered materialists in the core group of liberal democracies in Western Europe, North America and Japan.

The question now arises as to why this value shift should be regarded as a globalizing trend. The answer is that it contributes to many of the developments discussed above. In materialist value-conflicts the key issue is the role of the state and the way in which it represents the interests of one class or another. Here the state is the focus of political attention and its structures will be extended insofar as political parties can enhance their support by so doing. In post-materialist politics the state is problematic: the new right regards it as a transgressor on individual freedoms and a distorter of markets; the new left views it as an agency of rampant materialism and a means for the juridificational control of populations and their minorities. More importantly post-materialism focuses political attention on trans-societal issues, the planetary problems discussed above. It indicates such phenomenologically globalizing items as 'the individual', 'life', 'humanity', and 'the earth' that indicate the universality of the condition of the inhabitants of the planet rather than the specific conditions of their struggle with an opposing class about the ownership of property or the distribution of rewards.

CONCLUSION: A GLOBAL POLITY?

In a similar way to the previous chapter, Table 5.1 attempts an assessment of the state of play in political globalization by comparing an ideal-typical globalized polity with the current state of affairs in each of the areas considered in this chapter. A critical and striking feature of political globalization is that it does not in any area exhibit the extreme level of globalization found, for example, in financial markets. Political globalization is most advanced in the areas of international relations and political culture. However, the state remains highly resistant, largely sovereign and a critical arena for problem solving. A possible explanation is that politics is a highly territorial activity and that the organized nation-state is the most effective means for establishing sovereignty over territory that human beings have yet devised. Globalization is a process with a spatial referent but that paradoxically threatens territorial sovereignty. The state might therefore just be the final bastion of resistance to globalizing trends and the key indicator of their ultimate effectivity. If states survive globalization then it cannot be counted the force that it currently appears to be.

The undermining of the state, and indeed such disétatization as has already occurred, must, on the arguments offered in this chapter, be counted as a cultural development. The theorem that material exchanges localize, power exchanges internationalize, and symbolic exchanges globalize can thus receive a good measure of confirmation. The expansion of the nation-state/international relations system organized the territorial surface of the planet with political entities of a single type. That process contributed to globalization but it was not truly globalizing because it also maintained borders and barriers to social intercourse between its inhabitants. These borders are now being subverted by transcendent cultural items that will not respect them because they can be transmitted by symbolic media. The spread of liberal democracy and of post-materialist values is not a *sui generis* development in each society where they occur but are transmitted from one society to another. Those who doubt the effectivity of culture might wish to compare the bloody and violent revolutions

Table 5.1 An inventory of political globalization

Dimension	Ideal-typical pattern of globalization	Current state of affairs
State sovereignty	Absence of sovereign states. Multiple centres of power at global, local and intermediate levels.	Crisis and attenuation of the state. Evidence of aggregation and decentralization of state powers.
Focus of problem-solving activity.	Local issues in the context of the global community.	Increasing focus on local-global nexus but societal community probably still paramount.
International organizations	Powerful; predominant over national organizations.	Multiplying rapidly but relatively powerless.
International relations	Fluid and multicentric.	Superpower system attenuating.
Political culture	Common and planetary transcendence of étatocentric value-commitments.	Advance of liberal democracy/ postmaterialism.

that established nation-states from the seventeenth to the nineteenth century with the almost bloodless coups and 'velvet revolutions' that have occurred in the last third of the twentieth. These suggest that the prospect of complete political globalization is a genuine possibility.

6

The new world chaos: cultural globalization

There will be no 'there' any more. We will all be here.
Advertisement for MCI Telecommunications

The previous chapters make the claim that globalization proceeds most rapidly in contexts in which relationships are mediated through symbols. Economic globalization is therefore most advanced in the financial markets that are mediated by monetary tokens and to the extent that production is dematerialized, and political globalization has proceeded to the extent that there is an appreciation of common planetary values and problems rather than commitments to material interests. The chapters also make the supplementary argument that material and power exchanges in the economic and political arenas are progressively becoming displaced by symbolic ones, that is by relationships based on values, preferences and tastes rather than by material inequality and constraint. On these arguments globalization might be conceived as an aspect of the progressive 'culturalization' of social life.

While it is clearly not the case that culture, as an arena differentiated from economics and politics, has ever been totally globalized it has nevertheless shown a greater tendency towards globalization than either of the other two arenas. This is particularly evident in the area of religion. For many centuries, the great universalizing religions of the world, Buddhism, Christianity, Confucianism, Islam and Hinduism offered adherents an exclusivist and generalizing set of values and allegiances that stood above both state and economy. In the medieval world, for example, Christendom was conceived as the kingdom of God on earth and Islam has always been conceived as a social community of material and political interests that supersedes the state. Indeed, in the thirteenth and fourteenth centuries these two theocratic units came into generalized conflict over the possession of one of their common sacred sites. These religions in particular have had a globalizing sense of mission in which they sought to convert those defined as heathen or infidel by whatever constraint was possible. One strategy was to align themselves with expansive empires that had global ambitions (e.g. the Arabian, British, Holy Roman, and Ottoman empires) and thus to export the belief system beyond its original point of adoption.

The great universalizing religions have generally been threatened or eclipsed by modernization and the rise of capitalism. But the emergence of the liberal-democratic state and of the capitalist economic system also carried with them universalizing values. The state carried a set of commitments to democracy, citizenship, patriotism and welfare, while capitalism carried commitments to instrumental rationality, acquisitiveness, individualism and the privacy of person and property. During the twentieth century the conflicts between the various aspects of these value-systems were played out in the context of the equally universalizing and often expansionist politico-economic ideologies of Communism, Conservatism, Fascism, Liberalism and Socialism. Like Christianity and Islam, these claimed global relevance, and their adherents campaigned and activized in order to establish them as the sole principle for the organization of individual values and preferences and for the legitimation of social organization across the planet.

However, much as we have done in the previous chapters, we must lay to rest a misconception that might arise out of this introductory discussion. The current accelerated phase of globalization does not refer to the triumph and sovereign domination of any one of these 'metanarratives' (Lyotard 1984) but rather to their dissipation. A globalized culture is chaotic rather than orderly – it is integrated and connected so that the meanings of its components are 'relativized' to one another but it is not unified or centralized. The absolute globalization of culture would involve the creation of a common but hyperdifferentiated field of value, taste, and style opportunities, accessible by each individual without constraint for purposes either of self-expression or consumption. Under a globalized cultural regime Islam would not be linked to particular territorially based communities in the Middle East, North Africa and Asia, but would be universally available across the planet and with varying degrees of 'orthodoxy', as indeed it has tended to become. Likewise in the sphere of political ideology, the apparently opposed political values of private property and power-sharing might be combined to establish new ideologies of economic enterprise, as indeed they have. A globalized culture admits a continuous flow of ideas, information, commitment, values and tastes mediated through mobile individuals, symbolic tokens and electronic simulations.

These flows, as Featherstone (1990: 6) argues, give a globalized culture a particular shape. First, it links together previously encapsulated and formerly homogeneous cultural niches forcing each to relativize itself to others. This relativization may take the form of either a reflexive self-examination in which fundamental principles are reasserted in the face of threatening alternatives or the absorption of some elements of other cultures. Second, it allows for the development of genuinely transnational cultures not linked to any particular nation-state-society which may be either novel or syncretistic. Appadurai's increasingly influential argument about the global cultural economy (1990) identifies several of the important fields in which these developments take place. The fields are identified by the suffix 'scape', that is they are globalized mental pictures of the social world perceived from the flows of cultural objects. The flows include: ethnoscapes, the distribution of mobile individuals (tourists, migrants, refugees, etc.); technoscapes, the distribution of technology; finanscapes, the distribution of capital; mediascapes, the distribution of information; and ideoscapes, the distribution of political ideas and values (e.g. freedom, democracy, human rights). Some of these flows have been discussed in the previous chapters and others will be discussed here but we begin by examining what Appadurai might have called 'sacriscapes', the distribution of religious ideas and values.

FUNDAMENTALISM AND ECUMENISM

As is indicated in the above introduction, the claims of universalistic religions that the world was created by a single God and
that humanity is a common form of existence in relation to that
God is a primary long-run driving force in the direction of globalization. It leads to the argument that humanity constitutes a single
community that disvalues geographical localities and political
territories. Among the universalizing religions the derivative
Abrahamic faiths of Christianity and Islam have proved the most
effective globalizers because of their missions of proselytization
and conversion. This is most explicit in Islam. The earthly objective of Islam is the establishment of a community of the faithful
(*Umma*), which is ruled hierocratically, in which practices specified by the Quran are followed to the letter, and which engages
in a holy struggle (*Jihad*) against unbelievers (Turner 1991: 169).
The expansion of the Arab and Ottoman empires from the twelfth
through the fifteenth centuries under the aegis of this theology
not only placed the 'nations' they conquered under a unified
cultural system but brought Islam into contact with Christianity
and forced some measure of relativization on each faith and its
associated culture. Indeed the failure of Christendom successfully
to control its Holy Land and its incapacity to missionize beyond
Europe may have contributed to the Protestant reformation and
thereby to a further spurt in the Western globalization process.

For many that process begins in the highly universalistic
though exclusivist seed-bed faith of Judaism. As Long (1991)
indicates, Judaism could not itself promote globalization because
its particularisms (especially the covenant between God and his
chosen people and the notion of a promised land) were so intense
and because it had no mission of conversion. The universalisms
contributed by it to Christianity and Islam were, however, criti-
cally important. These included the ideas that there was indeed
a singular and abstract God, a single value-reference for every
person in the world, and that this God proposed a single set of
legal and moral laws. Only these universalistic elements were
adopted by early Christianity, which in fact syncretized Judaic
monotheism with Greek humanism (hence the deification of
Christ) and Roman imperialism (Strange 1991). Indeed two critical elements in the expansion of Christianity were its use of
Greek, the *lingua franca* of the period, and its eventual alignment
with the Roman imperial dynasty.

Thereafter, and for the next thousand or so years, Christianity ceased to be a purely cultural movement and more closely approximated a political ideology. Its globalizing consequence was the legitimation of the incorporation of tribal peasants into large-scale political systems. It achieved this by specifying that social order was ordained and that the relationship between any individual and God had to be mediated through a priestly hierarchy. Under this religious regime, the conscience was truly collective and the earthly orientation was almost entirely towards the maintenance of internal societal order. It was not until after the establishment of the Iberian colonies in the Americas in the sixteenth century that Christianity, or Catholicism as it had become, again began to develop a conversion mission (Muldoon 1991). By that time, however, a newer and far more important globalizing religious force had emerged.

The Protestant Reformation was critical in the development of Western globalizing trends in two important respects. First, Christianity had always fudged the issue of the relationship between the powers of state and church (e.g. in the very notion of Christendom) so that there had been a long series of jurisdictional conflicts between kings and the popes to whom they nominally owed spiritual allegiance. The Reformation resolved this dispute either by subordinating the church to the state, as in England, or by secularizing the state, as in the USA and republican France. The state could now rely on the political legitimations of nationalism or liberalism rather than religious legitimation and the stage was thus set for the emergence and enhancement of its powers which was itself the prerequisite for internationalization (see Chapter 5).

Second, medieval Christianity also maintained some significant particularisms insofar as some people were regarded as closer to God than others (e.g. monarchs received their tenancies directly from God) and insofar as relationships to God had to be mediated through priests. Protestantism raised universalism to a new level by asserting the possibility of a direct relationship between every individual and God by the mechanisms of prayer, conscience and faith. It therefore asserted that all were equal in relation to God and that salvation did not depend on one's inclusion within a religiously ordered political community. Any inhabitant of the planet could now become a Christian simply by an act of faith so that by the nineteenth century Protestant

missionaries were fanning out across the planet to give its inhabitants the good news. Catholic missionaries were not far behind.

Thus the religion, whether Protestant or reformed Catholic,
that is associated with Western modernity is highly secularized
and privatized. It specifies that the morals of state and economic
action, for example, are governed not by general and public
principles but by the consciences of their individual practitioners.
War and economic exploitation can thus equally be condoned
because Christianity assumes that politicians and business leaders
have exercised an individual moral calculus in advance of the act.
Insofar as capitalism and the nation-state are crucial configur-
ations within globalization, the Protestant reformation liberates
them then from cultural constraint. But Beyer (1990) encourages
us to stress that Protestantism carries with it its own positive
contribution to globalization. Under medieval Christianity or
Islam a territorial distinction could be maintained between good
and evil, the saved and the damned, or the believers and the
infidels – the good lived in a common space inside the community
and the bad outside. To the extent that belief or goodness is
a matter of individual conscience, the fact that a person is a
neighbour need not imply that they are as morally sound as
oneself. The community of the faithful is dotted across the world
and not confined to a locality, and so too are the morally feckless.
In embracing individualism, Protestantism thus challenges spatial
constraints.

Until the third quarter of the twentieth century, religion
under Western modernity followed the individualized Protestant
pattern. Traditionally sociologists interpreted it under what has
become known as secularization theory, the thesis that religious
beliefs and practices are trending towards separation in time and
space (i.e. only in church and only on Sunday), that they are
decreasingly oriented to narrative mythologies and more to
abstract philosophical principles, and that individuals are becoming more non-religious or even irreligious. Two related empirical
developments are now challenging secularization theory: first,
there are signs that in many societies the decline in religious
beliefs is stabilizing or even reversing (see Duke and Johnson
1989); and second, a wave of fundamentalist transformation is
revitalizing the old universal religions.

The sources of these developments are modernization/post-
modernization and globalization (Lechner 1989, 1992; Robertson
1992: 164–81). From its classical beginnings, sociology has always

asserted that modernization disrupts the solidarity of meaning systems because it isolates individuals and families, rends communities, and denies the relevance of the sacred and of substantive values. Millenarian movements have often sought to resist the excesses of modernization but have failed in the face of its capacity to provide both short-run, individualized material gratifications and the promise of an ever-expanding future of material growth. However, postmodernization (Harvey 1989; Crook *et al.* 1992) has displaced even the certainties offered by modernization insofar as the pathways to material success are no longer clearly defined and insofar as its collective social arrangements (classes, Fordist enterprises, states) are attenuating. Postmodernization therefore accelerates the search for a single, often mythologized truth that can reference all social mores and practices. Fundamentalist religious and ethnic movements thus respond to the hyperdifferentiating tendencies of postmodernization. Lechner (1990: 79) describes them as: 'A value-oriented, antimodern, dedifferentiating form of collective action – a sociocultural movement aimed at reorganizing all spheres of life in terms of a particular set of absolute values.'

Globalization also contributes both directly and indirectly to the world-wide development of fundamentalism. Its indirect effects are constitituted neither as simple cultural mimesis nor as the syncretization of a single set of common elements from different traditions but because it carries the discontents of modernization and postmodernization to religious traditions that might previously have remained encapsulated. As Robertson phrases it, religious systems are obliged to relativize themselves to global postmodernizing trends. This relativization can involve an embracement of the postmodernizing pattern, an abstract and humanistic ecumenism, but it can also take the form of a rejective search for original traditions.

However, there are also direct effects. Lechner (1991: 276–8) shows that globalization has characteristics that are independent of modernity and that force religious and other forms of relativization. These include:

- the universalization of Western cultural preferences that require local particularisms to be legitimated in their terms (e.g. the Islamic *Umma* must now be defended and reinforced in the face of Western claims about human rights, market democracy, and the position of women);

- the globalization of the nation-state-society that denies the legitimacy of superior allegiances to a church or its Gods;
- the secularization and abstraction of law as the basis for social order;
- the establishment of the fact that the world is pluralistic and choice-driven, that there is not a single and superior culture.

However, fundamentalism is not the only possible religious response to globalizing and postmodernizing pressures. During the 1960s and 1970s Christianity experienced an ecumenical movement in which dialogue between its denominations and ecclesia increased in an attempt to discover common principles and commitments and with a view to unification. Indeed some denominations, notably the individualistic Protestant ones, did amalgamate. The general consequence was a further abstraction and thus secularization and privatization of religious belief that many 'traditionalists' found both threatening and offensive. So this ecumenical movement itself promoted such fundamentalist schisms as the Lefevbre group of Tridentinist Catholics. However, the most important revitalizing, fundamentalist religious movements were much larger in scale and we can now review the globalizing aspects of some of the most important of these.

Perhaps the most pressing example for sociological analysis has been the development of what is known as the New Christian Right in the USA. In fact this is a loose term for a coalition of genuine fundamentalist protestants with traditionalists from the Episcopalian and Catholic churches that seeks directly to influence politics in the direction of reduced moral and sexual permissiveness, explicit references at the state level to Christian symbols, 'creationist' education, the criminalization of abortion, and a repressive attitude to crime and other forms of 'deviance'. The core of the movement is a Protestant group called the Moral Majority led by Jerry Falwell, which parallels Paisleyite Protestantism in Northern Ireland and Fred Nile's 'Call to Australia' movement. Although its membership is small, its effects are magnified by the successes of Televangelism, which mass mediates the fundamentalist messages of such charismatic figures as Billy Graham, Oral Roberts, Jimmy Swaggart, and Jim Bakker, although their messages are seldom directly political. The New Christian Right made a significant contribution to the establishment and the ideological tinge of the Reagan-Bush presidencies of 1980–91, and a much more direct one by means of the Robertson presidential candidacy in 1987. More importantly, evangelical broadcasting has found its way beyond the borders of the USA by means of short-wave radio and satellite television. The three largest international Christian broadcasters produce 20,000 hours of programming a week in 125 languages, which makes them the largest single element in transnational broadcasting (Haddon 1991: 232, 240). While it is difficult to assess its impact, such broadcasting can do little but enhance the conversion work of new wave American fundamentalist Protestant missionaries in Latin America and Africa.

However, there is no better example of the relativizing effect of globalization than the fundamentalist revival in Islam that began in the 1970s. Until that time the Islamic world, as Turner (1991) notes, had been dominated by the issues introduced by secular nationalistic and socialist political movements. However, Western modernization in either its capitalistic (e.g. Libya, Iran, Pakistan) or Marxist (e.g. Algeria, Egypt) forms failed to deliver either material benefits or a coherent system of meanings. Indeed rapid industrialization and urbanization appeared to offer only radical inequality between the populace and the politically dominant elite. Islamic fundamentalisms, particularly those associated with the Iranian cleric, the Ayotollah Khomeini, the dictatorship of General Zia-ul-Haq in Pakistan, the Islamic revival in Malaysia, and the activities of the Moslem brotherhood and Hezbollah in the Middle East, all mark a rejection of Western modernization and secularism. They call for 'Islamization', the creation of a hierocratic *Umma* in which education centres on the holy book, in which the economic system is oriented to redistribution rather than to acquisition, in which Sharia law displaces secular law, and in which cultural products (music, television programmes) are puritanized (Turner 1991: 175). At the same time globalization has made a pan-Islamic movement possible in which transfers of money, military intervention, terrorism, mass-mediated messages, and *hadj* pilgrims connect the elements of a world community.

Two Far-Eastern fundamentalist movements are also significant in the context of globalization. At one level, the Japanese Buddhist revivalism known as Soka Gakkai (Shupe 1991) is classically fundamentalist: it emphasizes traditional rural values; it calls for the revitalization of the state in the face of occidental decadence; and it is militantly evangelistic. At another it has a: 'global aspiration to become the world religion that will usher in a

war-free millenium' (Shupe 1991: 191) that it is seeking to promote by taking an international stance in promoting nuclear dis-
armament. Soka Gakkai owed its early success in the 1940s and
1950s to its programme of national revitalization but it has had
a very considerable recent expansion in response to its global
outreach. Even more globalized in its theology is Sun Myung
Moon's Unification Church, a Christian fundamentalism that originated in Korea in the 1950s and spread to the West in the 1970s
(Barker 1991). In its own terms it aims to restore, at one fell
swoop, the Kingdom of God on Earth. This community will be a
theocracy with the following characteristics:

> [It] will have no place for atheistic communism; there
> will be no pornography; sexual activity will be confined
> to marriage; crime will have been drastically reduced ...
> wars will be eradicated; exploitation ... will be a thing
> of the past; racial prejudice will have disappeared – and
> there will be no need for passports.
>
> (Barker 1991: 202)

In connecting the local to the global, Moon's theology appears
almost to reify sociological theories of globalization. Unification
is not to be the consequence of grand political action but of
changes in the hearts and the family practices of individuals. To
ensure compatibility and God-centredness Moon matches
spouses. To the extent that God-centred families are created,
global unification will proceed.

COSMOPOLITANIA

In its embrace of secularization theory, sociology took the view
that the 'irrational' influence of religion on society would be
tamed within an enlightened modernity. A second aspect of social
life which might equally be regarded as threatening and irrational
is ethnicity and its political expression, nationalism. From one
point of view ethnic allegiances and commitments might be held
to have been 'civilized' within the rationalistic structures of the
nation-state but a more compelling argument might be that
the nation-state actually unleashed the forces of nationalism
into the world by harnessing ethnicity to the state project
(Hobsbawm 1992).

In the premodern world, ethnicity was a taken-for-granted
component of identity associated with tribalism – the

Durkheimian notion of a mechanically solidaristic segment is
an appropriate formal conceptualization. It was also politically
unproblematic because there was no social technology that successfully could connect the large-scale political systems of empires
and feudal monarchies and large-scale religious cultures with local
practices. Medieval culture was in fact highly disunified so that
political units were loose confederations of minority ethnic affili-
ations and the large-scale European continental empires could
only survive as long as ethnic diversity was tolerated. Local segments owed formal allegiance to the centre and owed levies of
troops and taxes to it but economic activity and cultural
expression in particular were organized on a local basis. Moreover
territory was not formally allocated as ethnicities flowed into each
other at the boundaries.

The connection between ethnie and nation is a deliberate
human construction by rising political classes seeking to displace
the feudal autarchy. From the end of the eighteenth century there
were specific attempts across Europe and in other parts of the
world to raise national consciousness in favour of that new and
modern form of political organization, the nation-state. Anderson's (1983) Marxist interpretation of nations as 'imagined
communities', in contradistinction to the 'real communities' of
class, has become an orthodox conceptualization in this regard.
Hobsbawm (1992: 188) argues that the objective of early nationalist movements was to invent a coincidence between four reference
points, people (ethnie)-state-nation-government, that is between
a common identity, a political system, a community and an administration. To these we can also add the important component of
territory, especially insofar as nationalism sought to establish the
exclusive occupation of a territory by the nation. However, this
nationalism was almost always ideological in character because
there was seldom an exact homology between the five reference
points. Only such very extreme forms of nationalism as German
Fascism could seek an exact correspondence by trying to incorporate external components of the ethnie and eliminating internal
minorities. Hobsbawm (1992: 186) estimates that not more than
a dozen of the 180 or so contemporary nation-states coincide
with a single ethnic or linguistic group. Hall would think this an
over-estimate: 'Modern nations are all cultural hybrids' (1992b:
297, italics deleted).

The political and intellectual elites that led the nationalist
challenge engaged in a series of ideological practices that sought

to represent the nation as a social, spatial and historical fact that is real, continuous and meaningful. Hall (1992b: 293–5) outlines five such practices:

- They told stories or histories of the nation indicating commonalities of experience, of triumph and struggle. Among a multitude of examples we can mention stories of the American West, the Irish struggle against famine and British absentee landlords, the Great Trek of the Boers, and Australian military defeat at Gallipoli. These stories give people a sense of a common and continuous heritage.
- They make assertions about national character, about British fair play, or Japanese honourability, or Chinese industry and respect for authority, or Canadian decency, or Irish martyrdom, or Australian mateship. A national character gives a sense of timelessness to the nation that is independent of history.
- They invent new patterns of ritual, pageantry and symbolism that give collective expression to the nation. These include flags, heroes, systems of national honours, special days, national ceremonies and so on. Some elites, Israel and Ireland are examples, invent or revive languages.
- They establish foundational myths and legends that locate the nation 'outside' history and give it a quasi-sacred character as well as a sense of originality or non-derivativeness. Examples include the Camelot stories of the English, the German revival of teutonic mythology, the Rastafarianism of Jamaicans, and the purported connections between modern and ancient Greece.
- They promote ideas of common breeding or even racial purity. The obvious example is the Nazi promotion of the idea of a German *Volk*, but the British speak of themselves as the island race and Malays as Bumiputras (sons of the soil).

It must be stressed that these practices are evident not only in the emergence of the nineteenth-century European nation-states but in the contemporary attempts of emerging nations to free themselves from Western political and economic imperialism. Foster (1991) notes the promotion of ideologies of *kastom* (i.e. custom) in Pacific island nations that gives an anti-Western emphasis to mystical wisdom and social and environmental harmony but is actually built upon Western conceptions of the 'noble savage'.

The last example should tell us that nationalism is both a globalized and a globalizing phenomenon. It is one of the components of culture that has been transmitted around the globe as part of the process of 'internationalization' discussed in Chapter 5. The establishment of nation-states everywhere provides a basis on which societies can be connected with one another. But nationalism carries with it a broader political culture that, as we have seen, is also subject to widespread adoption. This culture includes a commitment to rational and dispassionate administration, to political representation and accountability, and to steering in the direction of enhanced collective material welfare.

At one level the current acceleration of globalization might be seen as destabilizing in relation to ethnicity. The previous chapters discuss the increasing integration of economic processes and the increasing interconnectedness of political practices, and the subsequent sections of this chapter discuss the emergence of a common global lifestyle and the rapid mediation of ideas by electronic communication and personal mobility. One might ask how it is possible for ethnic identification to survive such an onslaught. To answer this question, one must bear in mind a point stressed throughout this book that globalization does not necessarily imply homogenization or integration. Globalization merely implies greater connectedness and de-territorialization. The possibility arises therefore of an increased measure of ethnic pluralism but in which ethnicities are not tied to any specific territory or polity.

We are now in a position to summarize the impact of globalization on ethnicity and nationhood (see Arnason 1990; Hall 1992b).

- Globalization is, in general, a differentiating as well as a homogenizing process. It pluralizes the world by recognizing the value of cultural niches and local abilities.
- Importantly, it weakens the putative nexus between nation and state releasing absorbed ethnic minorities and allowing the reconstitution of nations across former state boundaries. This is especially important in the context of states that are confederations of minorities.
- It brings the centre to the periphery. Insofar as globalization is sourced in Western modernity, it introduces

possibilities for new ethnic identities to cultures on the periphery. The vehicles for this cultural flow are electronic images and affluent tourism.

- It also brings the periphery to the centre. An obvious vehicle is the flow of economic migrants from relatively disadvantaged sectors of the globe to relatively advantaged ones. It is also accomplished insofar as the mass media engage in a search for the exotic to titillate audiences in search of variety. Previously homogeneous nation-states have, as a consequence, moved in the direction of multi-culturalism.

Hall (1992b), drawing on Robins, identifies two possible adaptive responses on the part of ethnic groups to these globalizing trends, translation and tradition, that parallel developments in religion. Translation is a syncretistic response in which groups that inhabit more than one culture seek to develop new forms of expression that are entirely separate from their origins. Tradition is ethnic fundamentalism, an attempt to rediscover the untainted origins of an ethnic group in its history. Tradition involves a search for the certainties of the past in a postmodern world where identity is associated with lifestyle and taste and is therefore constantly shifting and challengeable. Paradoxically the search for tradition can contribute to this postmodern ambience by mixing the symbolic contents of the past into the present as everyday life becomes an historical and ethnic Disneyland.

Perhaps the best example of a translationist ethnicity is the emergence of the new identity in the 1960s and 1970s signified by the term 'black' (Hall 1992b: 308–9). In the USA this involved not only the translation of the disrupted and irrevocably mixed tribal identities that slaves had carried with them from Africa but also the translation of a class identity into an ethnic one that could become a source of pride. Although there has always been some ambivalence between translationist and traditionalist strategies, signified by the term 'Afro-American', only the former could allow black Americans both to assert their identity and to divest themselves of their association with the urban lumpenproletariat, the outcome of their migration to the Northern industrial cities in the early twentieth century. Black identity can also offer other political advantages. In Britain, for example, it has allowed coalition across populations with origins in the Caribbean, South Asia and Africa. Here again though the traditionalistic elements of Rastafarianism and Hindu and Islamic revivalism also inter-weave the process.

Another syncretistic ethnogenesis is the emergence of Quebec nationalism, which Hobsbawm describes as: 'a combination of intensified petty-bourgeois linguistic nationalism with mass future shock' (1992: 171). Québécois culture had survived since the seventeenth century on the basis of being ignored as too trouble-some by the Anglophone power centres and its own unification around the Catholic Church and local political patronage. In the 1960s and 1970s Quebec was penetrated by the global currents of industrialization and secularization and it also received an influx of 'third language' migrants anxious, in a globalized world, to learn the *lingua anglia*. The emerging nationalism was frequently defensive, relativized in self-references to 'white niggers' and claimed associations with the colonized third world, but often securely confident – the Quebec revolution had been a 'quiet revolution'. Above all, though, it laid claim to a new identity. The new Quebec society did not regard itself as a Parisien colony. Indeed until the late 1960s the European French regarded Québécois as primitives. Rather, it claimed to represent a fusion of European origins with North American experience of the culti-vated with the rational. Quebec was probably the first of many such nationalisms. Other examples, often with similar ambiv-alences about nation-state formation, include Bangladesh, Bougainville, Catalonia, Eritrea, Flanders, Kashmir, Kurdistan, Lombardy, Palestine, Scotland, Tamil Elam and Wales.

A rich source of traditionalistic ethnic revivals is the dismem-berment of the state-socialist confederations of Eastern Europe and Asia that began in the late 1980s. Two interpretations are possible of the emergence of such entities as Estonia, Slovakia, 'greater Serbia', Bosnia-Hercegovina, Kazakhstan, Moldavia, and Kirghizia. Hall (1992b: 312–13) views them as a continuation of the nationalistic movement that began at the end of the eight-eenth century: 'These new would-be 'nations' try to construct states that are unified in both ethnic and religious terms, and to create political entities around homogeneous cultural identities' (1992: 312). By contrast, for Hobsbawm the attempt is bound to fail: 'That ethno-linguistic separation provides no sort of basis for a stable, in the short run even for a roughly predictable, ordering of the globe is evident in 1992 from the merest glance at the large region situated between Vienna and Trieste in the West and Vladivostock in the East' (1992: 184). For him the creation of these small states is merely a step in the creation of a world of nations organized regionally and globally rather than on a state basis. He predicts moves towards supranationalism and infranationalism, that is towards political and economic organization on a continental or global scale and to the organization of culture and identity on a local scale. The evidence is the ambivalence with which emerging nations approach statehood – Scotland and Catalonia seek independence not within the framework of a new state but within a new relationship with the EU, and the Baltic states no sooner are detached from the Soviet Union than they are seeking membership of NATO and the EU.

In summary the effect of globalization on ethnicity is to revive it and to differentiate it from politics and economics. It enables the view that all ethnic identities are legitimate and not merely those successful ones that managed to establish states in the nineteenth century. In some instances this means the disruption of confederations of nations (e.g. Canada, Czechoslovakia, UK, USSR, Yugoslavia). However, all political entities are coming to be regarded as legitimately, even positively multicultural. Developments in the two fundamentals of sex and food can confirm this. All the evidence suggests that ethnicity is a declining barrier to love and marriage, a development that nationalistic barriers cannot conceivably survive. Moreover recipes for food consumption are becoming decreasingly localized both in terms of the diversity of so-called 'ethnic' restaurants and in the heterogeneity of domestic consumption. The postmodernization as well as globalization of ethnicity, that is its decoupling from locality, is confirmed by the development of ethnic theme parks in Japan to allow foreign tourism at home. They include 'The German Happiness Kingdom', 'Canadian World', 'Venice of Japan', 'Holland Village', 'Niigata Russian Village' and 'Cannonball City', a recreation of life in the USA (*Economist* 22–28/1/94).[1]

CONSUMER SOVEREIGNTY

The above discussion of religion and ethnicity should confirm that it is possible to over-simplify and thereby to over-demonize the process of globalization. We have seen that globalization can revive particularisms insofar as it relativizes them and insofar as it releases them from encapsulation by the nation-state-society. But globalization does not simply imply a revival of difference. It implies a complex interweave of homogenizing with differentiating trends. In this section we concentrate on the homo-genizing trends that are summed up in the phrase 'global consumer culture' and for which such value-laden terms as 'Americanization', 'Western cultural imperialism' and 'Coca-colonization' are often employed, and not without good reason. These terms imply that the consumer culture that was developed in the USA in the middle of the twentieth century has been mass mediated to all other parts of the world.

We need to stress that consumer culture means more than simple consumption (Featherstone 1991). An interest in consumption is historically and cross-societally universal. However, in a consumer culture the items consumed take on a symbolic and not merely a material value. It arises in societies where powerful groups, usually those seeking to accumulate capital, in caricature, encourage consumers to 'want' more than they 'need'. Indeed such groups will seek to confound the meanings of these two terms. Under a consumer culture, consumption becomes the main form of self-expression and the chief source of identity. It implies that both material and non-material items, including kinship, affection, art, and intellect become commodified, that is their value is assessed by the context of their exchange, rather than the context of their production or use. An advanced or postmod-ernized consumer culture experiences hypercommodification (Crook *et al.* 1992) in which minute differences between products or minute improvements in them can determine variations in demand, and in which consumption is differentiated on the basis of the signifiers known as 'brand names'. Here consumption, or more precisely a capacity to consume, is itself reflexively con-sumed. This tendency is captured in such terms as 'taste', 'fashion' and 'lifestyle' that become key sources of social differentiation, displacing class and political affiliation. The consumer culture is created through the advertising and simulatory effects of the mass media. In its original form it was probably a deliberate creation[2] but under postmodernized conditions it is 'hypersimulated' (Baudrillard 1988), having a life of its own that is beyond the control of any particular group.

Because it is symbolically mediated, consumer culture liberates values and preferences from particular social and geographical locations and indeed invalidates the social and political structures of modernity including states. It does so by undermining the cultural classifications of modernity, technically by declassifying or dedifferentiating culture. Bourgeois domination might have been legitimated by its claim to have special knowledge of cultural standards in art, morality and justice but in a consumer culture these standards merely become some of a range of opinions that can be accepted or rejected at will. Indeed the delegitimation of such standards has meant a more widespread and popular dissemination of what previously would have been regarded as high or elite cultural products. To give just one highly globalized and postmodernized example, the 'three tenors' concert of 1992 linked operatic music to the popular sport of soccer, set it up as spectacle as much as a concert, and marketed it by the mass media to a huge global audience.

If the original American version of consumer culture depended on mass mediated advertising and simulation that process has entered a global phase with the expansion of communications technologies beyond the nation-state-society (see the subsequent section of this chapter). The examples are numerous but a few may suffice to illustrate the point. In the 1930s the German car industry built a *Wagen* for its own *Volk* and the Model T and the Austin 7 were similarly conceived of as cars for the people of their respective nations, but now manufacturers build and market 'world cars', the latest from Ford appropriately called the 'Mondeo'. The 'many colours of Bennetton', stressed presumably because colour is one of the few minute variations offered in their standardized clothing products, Nike and Reebok casual shoes, and Levi jeans infuse global popular culture. The expansion of the products of major fashion houses into such downmarket but associated brands as Armani Emporium, DKNY, and YSL ape this global marketing strategy as well as illustrating postmodernizing declassification. A particular example of the local-global connection might be the way in which such peculiarly Australian products as Akubra hats, Drizabone wet weather gear, and Blundstone boots (not to mention Foster's lager) have become internationally recognized brands, but recognized because they are specifically Australian. In food and beverage products, global branding has been so effective that the examples are almost too obvious to mention: Coca-cola and its rival Pepsi are the paradigm case, now doing battle in China, the last sector of the globe that they have failed to dominate; McDonalds and its rivals, Pizza Hut, Sizzlers, and KFC fast-food restaurants engorge the world with vast quantities of sanitized and homogenized food; and kitchens are stocked, as occasionally are the walls of art galleries, with Campbell's soup, Pilsbury instant bread, and

Birds Eye frozen peas. Nor is global branding restricted to mass markets. Global yuppiedom is equally susceptible to the attractions of Rolex watches, Porsche cars, Luis Vuitton luggage, Chanel perfume, AGA kitchen stoves, Dom Perignon champagne, and Perrier mineral water.

Although sympathy for such a spread of popular culture has become unfashionable, the view from the Elysian heights may be a little clouded. Certainly one's diet would be homogenized if one ate every day at McDonalds but there are, for example, isolated and traditional Buddhist societies in the Himalayas whose diet consists almost entirely of barley porridge, barley bread, and barley beer, and anyone raised on English school dinners could hardly make claims for the tantalizing variety of that particular national dietary culture. This is to say that the globalization of popular culture has apparently paradoxical but actually consistent effects in simultaneously homogenizing and differentiating. Certainly it can homogenize across the globe in that what is available in any locality can become available in all localities but at any particular locality it increases the range of cultural opportunity. For example, New Yorkers would be in a sorry condition if the only wine they could drink was that produced in their own state. In fact that particular city, like many 'global cities' (King 1990b) offers a dazzling variety of consumption possibilities drawn from across the globe in terms not only of imported products but of imported cultural practices.

This leads us to consideration of another development that might be conceived to be positive. Throughout, this book has accepted Robertson's argument, contra Giddens, that globalization precedes modernization and is independent of it, and that it is therefore a long-term historical process. Consumption-based cultural globalization actually began in the nineteenth century but in the arena of elite or bourgeois culture. At that time, what previously had been courtly preferences in music and art trickled down to the *nouveaux riches* and they established public art galleries, museums and libraries, civic symphony orchestras, national opera, ballet and drama companies, and open and secular universities to institutionalize (and socialize the costs of) their newly found sense of taste. As capitalism expanded across the globe these cultural institutions were carried by its dominant class so that no new society and no newly industrialized society, even if state socialist, could regard itself as having an autonomous national culture without them. By the end of the nineteenth century, a global but mainly European cultural tradition had been established in which the same music, the same art and the same literature and science were equally highly regarded in many parts of the globe. Indeed, new methods of transportation allowed world tours by master practitioners and performers and allowed students to study at international centres of excellence, all of which served to consolidate a homogenized global high culture. However, popular culture remained nation-state specific until the development of cinematographic and electronic mass mediation. A long-term effect of these media has been to democratize culture because they refuse to respect the 'specialness' or auratic quality of high cultural products.

There are two broad views of the way in which consumer culture pervades the globe and invades and controls the individual. The most common explanation is one in which individual identity is conflated to culture. Capitalism transforms people into consumers by altering their self-images, their structure of wants, in directions that serve capitalist accumulation (e.g. Friedman 1990; Sklair 1991). This view is contestable in terms of the impressive example of Eastern Europe and the former Soviet Union where many, perhaps a majority, of the populations embraced consumer culture on the basis only of glimpses of life in the West and despite massive propaganda about the evils of consumerism. The 'velvet revolutions' of the late 1980s can be viewed as a mass assertion of the right to unlimited privatized consumption, a right which might also be viewed as a central issue in the third world.

A second and more interesting argument is Ritzer's view (1993) of consumer culture as an extension of the process of Western rationalization first identified by Weber. Weber had broadly been interested in the ways in which the rational calculability of capitalism was extended beyond material issues to human relationships, specifically those to do with production in its broadest sense of goal-attainment. Ritzer's view is that society, and thus the world, is afflicted by a process of 'McDonaldization': 'the process by which the principles of the fast-food restaurant are coming to dominate more and more sectors of American society as well as the rest of the world' (1993: 1, italics deleted). The principles are as follows (1993: 7–13):

- efficiency: McDonaldization compresses the time span and the effort expended between a want and its satisfaction;

- calculability: it encourages calculations of costs of money, time and effort as the key principles of value on the part of the consumer, displacing estimations of quality;
- predictability: it standardizes products so that consumers are encouraged not to seek alternatives;
- control of human beings by the use of material technology; this involves not only maximal deskilling of workers but control of consumers by means of queue control barriers, fixed menu displays, limited options, uncomfortable seats, inaccessible toilets, and 'drive-through' processing.

Clearly, to the extent that the social technology of McDonaldization can penetrate the globe and to the extent that it can induce consumers to enter premises, it can convert apparently sovereign consumers into docile conformists. McDonaldization of course travels with the restaurant chain that gave it its name. By the end of 1991 there were 12,000 of them and in that year for the first time it opened more outlets outside the USA (427) than inside (188). But the formula has been extended to other fast food brands (Burger King, Pizza Hut, Taco Bell), to more up-market restaurants (Sizzlers) and to the marketing of a wide range of products including car servicing (Mr Muffler, Jiffylube), financial services (H&R Block, ITP), childcare (Kinder Care, Kampgrounds of America), medical treatment, university education,[3] bakery products (Au Bon Pain), and many more (Ritzer 1993: 2–3). In summary, McDonaldization represents a reordering of consumption as well as production, a rationalization of previously informal and domestic practices, that pushes the world in the direction of greater conformity.

The paradox of McDonaldization is that in seeking to control, it recognizes that human individuals potentially are autonomous, a feature that is notoriously lacking in 'cultural dupe' or 'couch potato' theories of the spread of consumer culture. As dire as they may be, fast-food restaurants only take money in return for modestly nutritious and palatable fare. They do not seek to run the lives of their customers although they might seek to run their diets. They attract rather than coerce so that one can always choose not to enter. Indeed, advertising gives consumers the message, however dubious, that they are exercising choice.

It might be argued that consumer culture is the source of the increased cultural effectivity that is often argued to accompany globalization and postmodernization. Insofar as we have a consumer culture the individual is expected to exercise choice. Under such a culture, political issues and work can equally become items of consumption. A liberal-democratic political system might be the only possible political system where there is a culture of consumption precisely because it offers the possibility of election. But even a liberal democracy will tend to be Mc-Donaldized, that is leaders will become the mass mediated images of photo-opportunities and juicy one-liners, and issues will be drawn in starkly simplistic packages. Equally work can no longer be expected to be a duty or a calling or even a means of creative self-expression. Choice of occupation, indeed choice of whether to work at all, can be expected increasingly to become a matter of status affiliation rather than of material advantage.

SIGNS OF A GLOBAL CULTURE

Although globalization predates modernization, modernization in particular generates media that can permeate and dissolve boundaries between localities and between political entities and thus allow cultural transmission to take place at an increasingly rapid rate. Token money was an obvious and important medium that we have discussed at several points. It had several effects. First, it allowed trade between localities to be transacted across a wide and generalized range of products. The more trade was extended, the greater was the probability of geographical special-ization by product, which would further promote trade and so on. The global product market began to develop quite early. Second, it allowed capital to be translated into the exchangeable form of finance and also to be exported and invested across distances. The marketization of capital eroded localized, kinship-based concentrations of capital and allowed its accumulation on an ever widening scale.

However, other media were also significant in linking localit-ies. The development of military sailing vessels in the fifteenth and sixteenth centuries coupled with an increasing level of macro-climatic and geographical knowledge which their use required, increased the possibility of discovery and exploration as far as planetary limits would allow. This was but a first step in the liberation of the medium of transportation from the limits of animate power but it was genuinely significant. Although the Phoenicians, the Venetians and the Vikings had achieved much using human rowers, the distant contacts that they made could not be sustained precisely because of an insufficiently developed economy of energy. Only the multi-masted sailing vessel, the Spanish galleon, the British clipper, or the Chinese junk, could sustain a pattern of global economic colonization. Indeed, only such vessels could carry more people than the number needed to power them and thus move settlers from Europe *en masse* to the far-flung reaches of the globe. The medium received a further boost with the discovery and application of steam power. Not only did steam power further multiply the effectiveness of marine transport but it also enabled the conquest, by railways, of vast continental distances in the Americas, Africa, Australia and Siberia. The internal combustion, diesel and jet engines and their associated technologies clearly multiplied globalizing possibilities.

The third significant globalizing medium provided by modernization is electrical, electronic and photographic means for the communication of information. Transportation improvements could themselves improve communication by mail. However, perhaps the most significant event in nineteenth-century globalization occurred during the Crimean War of the 1850s when the war correspondent of *The Times*, a Mr Russell, was able to telegraph his reports instantly back to London for the first time, so that descriptions of the events were available a mere day or two after they happened. The rest, as they say, is history – by about the turn of the century communication could be achieved by telephone, by wireless, by cinematography, and even by television. Distant events could be known about, even 'witnessed' without leaving one's own locality.

A significant spurt of globalization occurred in the nineteenth century, partly as a consequence of the development of these transportation and communication media. The invention of the social technology of administration (and surveillance) allowed power to be extended across territories and their inhabitant populations in a direct and centralized way. The key location of power for any individual member of one of the new nation-states was no longer a local kinsman or potentate but a distant bureaucratic system. The hierarchical organization of bureaucracies could be extended across such territories by the use of reporting systems. So effective were these bureaucracies that trans-global colonial systems involving territories and populations many times greater than those of the colonizing power could be administered and thus controlled from the European centres.

The early twentieth century saw the development of media

machines using the complex technology of electricity and the opportunity for a truly symbolized form of globalization. The phonograph, the telephone, and the moving picture were the first such developments to attain widespread popularity but radio and television were also physically invented quite early in the century. Radio, the first true electronic mass medium, became well established in the 1920s and 1930s. Television began to penetrate mass markets only after the Second World War, both hailed and feared as a more powerful and pervasive medium than radio, with an even greater potential to affect the minds of those consuming its contents.

The most recent technological trends involve extensions and recombinations of the basic artefacts – telephone, record-and-playback machine, radio, and television. They can be summarized as follows:

- *Miniaturization*: All technologies have reduced in size. This is in part due to design criteria that apply in Japanese consumer electronics companies, which are pace-setters for the industry. Among these companies, Sony was the first effective miniaturizer when it bought out the patents of an American invention, the transistor, and built the portable radio. The trend applies to cassette players, disc players, TVs, telephones and computers. Miniaturization affects transmission as well as reception – a key factor in the satellite news broadcaster CNN's 'scoop' of Iraqi reactions to the attack on their territory by the USA and its allies in 1988 was the capacity of its journalists to set up a 'backpack' satellite transmission station in Baghdad.
- *Personalization*: There has historically been a general reduction of the scope of the audience for electronic mass communications. The music hall or the cinema could entertain several hundred, the television a family, but the PC is literally a 'personal computer', although it is not actually quite as personal as a lap-top computer, which is itself not quite as personal as a palm-top computer. The Sony 'Walkman' and its mimics represent the ultimate in personalized consumption – the sound becomes all-encompassing and internal.
- *Integration:* The various technologies of text, sound, visuals, and response via keyboard or microphone are progressively becoming integrated with one another. This

centres on the technology of the microchip which organizes computers. The microchip provides an enormous capacity to process information.

- *Diffusion:* Access to technologies of mass media is becoming more widespread in terms of both reception and transmission. The former is the consequence of the declining relative cost of receivers, the latter of such technological leaps as the exploration of space and fibre optics. Such diffusion implies not only that virtually every inhabitant of the planet has access to mass communications but an increasing range of choice within mass communications. It also implies it is now impossible to maintain national sovereignty in mass communications so long as the members of a society have access to satellite dishes.

- *Autonomization:* Fears that audiences might simply be the victims, or at least the passive receptors, of mass mediated information appear to be receding. Consumers have an increasing potential for autonomy insofar as: they have a greater choice of products (e.g. via cable and satellite TV); they have increased 'talk-back' capacity via telephones and interactive computer networks; they have increased access to production facilities via home recording equipment and community studios; and they can control the timing and content of what they watch and hear by means of compact discs, cassettes, and video cassettes.

All this technology originates in advanced capitalist societies as does much of its content. In terms of cultural globalization it has three principal effects. First, it exports what Sklair (1991) calls the 'culture-ideology of consumerism' from the centre to the periphery of the world-system. This is because most of the news, information, entertainment programming, sport, information and advertising flows in that direction (Anderson 1984; Hoskins and Mirus 1988; Mowlana 1985; Sklair 1991). Not only the programme producers but the advertising agencies and news agencies as well as the companies that manufacture consumer products are owned in advanced capitalist societies. Advertising, in particular, seeks to sell products by depicting idealized Western lifestyles, often under the universalizing themes of sex, status and the siblinghood of humanity – the world sings a hymn of harmony to a soft drink of doubtful nutritional value. They mimic the opportunities for simulation already given in soap operas, sitcoms and action thrillers.

Second, as well as absorbing new nations into what some might call the network of cultural imperialism, cultural flows via the mass media dissolve the internal boundaries of that network and help to knit it together. These cultural flows are primary examples of transnational connections, links between collective actors and individuals that subvert state frontiers. As we note above, satellite broadcasting in particular denies the possibility of national sovereignty over the airwaves. A specific consequence is that, insofar as much of the hardware is American-owned and much of the programming is American in origin, English is becoming the *lingua franca* of the global communications system. This has proved a particular problem for the territorially small nations of Europe but the failure of Euronews, a multilingual satellite news channel, to dent the market shares of CNN and Sky News that broadcast exclusively in English, indicates that English may well become the common public language of the globalized system and that vernaculars may be restricted to local-ized and domestic contexts.

However, the mass media knit the global culture together by means of content as well as by means of language. They do this not merely by offering common simulation opportunities but by magnifying global problems and global events. We can say, with appropriate apologies, that we now look at the world through global spectacles. When an American fighter pilot bombs a build-ing in Baghdad we are there with her seeing what she sees and war becomes a spectacle; the demolition of the Berlin wall, a major political event, becomes a rock concert; the Olympic games expands its range of sports to include artistic rather than athletic events, however kitsch (rhythmic gymnastics, synchronized swim-ming, freestyle skiing) in order to reach a wider global audience; and the 'A Team' can scarcely compare for thrills with the Tiananmen massacre of 1988 or Yeltsin's conquest of the Russian parliament in 1993. These media events are of a qualitatively different order from, say, the television coverage of the first human landing on the moon in 1968. They are deliberately constructed as stylized mass entertainments and they are, in Durkheimian terms, collective representations of global commitments to democracy, consumption, capitalism and a liberal tolerance of diversity.

The third globalizing effect of the mass media is the one originally noticed by McLuhan and argued further by Harvey

and by Giddens (see Chapter 3). Insofar as the mass media
convert the contents of human relationships into symbols or
tokens, they can connect people across great distances. So effective can this process become that communities of interest or
value-commitment can develop between people who have never
met, much less joined together in a political event. These are
elsewhere described as simulated communities or simulated
power blocs (Crook *et al.* 1992: 131–4) because they are based
on behavioural cues given only in the mass media. For example,
many women feel a sense of global sisterhood in relation to
patriarchal oppression even if they are not participants in the
women's movement. Further, insofar as symbols can be transmitted very rapidly, the compression of time eliminates the
constraints and therefore the social reality of space.

The influence of the telephone and television in this respect
is well established but the newest, and possibly the most effective
medium in accomplishing time-space compression is 'Internet', an
international network of direct links between computers. Internet
originated in the USA where it grew out of a merging of Local
Area Networks originally under military sponsorship. It is now
mainly an academic and research network but commercial organizations are beginning to use it to commodify information.
Internet is global[4] in its reach but not total in its coverage – it
has 15 million users, growing at a rate of 20–30 per cent every
three months. Internet still simulates global space, however,
because users need to conceptualize and find other 'places' in
order to use the information there. However, new hypermedia
software is now becoming available, under such names as World
Wide Web and Global Network Navigator, that will act as an
agent for the user, independently searching the network, finding
bits of information in different parts of it, combining them and
presenting them back to the user without any reference to space
(*Economist* 5–11/2/94). Equally, the software will render Internet
increasingly user-friendly and thus generalize its use. The chief
importance of such a development is that it will provide an
opportunity for the realization of simulated communities that can
now develop out of trans-global patterns of interaction. McLuhan's global village was perhaps misnamed because a village
without circuits of gossip would be strange indeed. Such globalized circuits of gossip are now becoming possible as is the reality
of McLuhan's vision.

GLOBETROTTERS AND JETSETTERS

In Chapters 2 and 3 we consider theoretical accounts that focus on the reorganization of Western phenomenologies of time and space at around the middle of the millenium. These accounts focus both on the way in which the mechanical clock disembedded time from natural diurnal and seasonal rhythms and the mapping of the globe dislocated space from place. Many were confronted with the fact that for the first time one's perceptions of the physical context were not limited to one's experience of it. The consequences were profound. Time could now be divided into segments and specific activities could be assigned to these different segments. In particular, public activity or 'work' could be separated in time from domestic activity which meant that to the extent that the latter was undemanding, it could be defined as leisure or recreation. Previously leisure could only occur in the ritual or carnivalesque atmospheres of feasts and holy days when whole days or weeks could be put aside. Now it was possible for leisure to become a universal and general expectation. Equally, as Marx tells us, work could be separated from home in space. For medievals and early moderns, travel was an unusual practice, undertaken in relation only to such biographically unusual events as military service, pilgrimage, trade or diplomacy. Partly because transport was slow, it was costly in terms of time. It was also regarded as risky, and those who travelled (explorers, crusaders, pilgrims) were regarded as courageous or saintly or perhaps foolish. The conceptualization of space normalized travel by routinizing travel between home and work and increasing notions of an opportunity for trade.

These phenomenological developments then, institutionalized two new and modern human possibilities as general features of social life, leisure and travel. This is not to suggest that in the early stages of capitalist industrialization either of them were generally accessible in any society. Rather it suggests that both were available to some sections of industrialized societies and that it was possible for any member of society to imagine themselves engaging in such an activity, in however utopian a fashion. These developments also gave rise to a new possibility, something that would have seemed quite bizarre to a medieval, the idea of travel for leisure, indeed of travel for pleasure or at least for its own sake. This possibility became a reality for the first time in the eighteenth century when aristocrats began to make what became known as the 'Grand Tour' (Turner and Ash 1975: 29–50). The Grand Tour was conceptualized as a civilizing process in which the elite from the cultural backwaters of England and France could rub up against the sumptuous splendour of post-Renaissance Italy. Accordingly it could last up to five years. In contrast, by the time the industrial bourgeoisies of England and the USA had cottoned on to the act in the late nineteenth century, both time and space had already shrunk, not least because of their time commitments to capitalist management. Tours lasted at most for a year but often for a few months and would attempt to take in Western and Central Europe in its entirety, within a more distant visual experience, rather than as a process of cultural immersion.

Nevertheless foreign travel in the nineteenth century was still regarded as a culturally uplifting experience rather than a pleasurable one, if only because it was conceived romantically to improve one's sense of the sublime (Urry 1990: 4). This was true even for the middle-class package holidays organized by Thomas Cook and later by American Express to such uplifting spots as Constantinople, Luxor, and tribal New Guinea.[5] Travel for pleasure emerged from a different context altogether as working-class families sought to escape the grimy drudgery of industrial cities. Although the development of British seaside resorts as working-class pleasure zones has attracted much sociological interest (Urry 1990; Shields 1991), the phenomenon was much more universal including such diverse examples as Coney Island, Bondi beach, and Varna on the Black Sea. Here 'holy days' were transformed into secular 'holidays' during which people became deeply committed to having a good time, and wishing others were with them, by doing things that they would not normally have done – breathing fresh air, eating sweet junk food, riding animals, wearing silly clothes, taking thrilling fairground rides, taking walks for no reason at all, and playing carnival gambling games. Equally, at around the turn of the nineteenth century, the more privileged sections of society established their own pleasure zones further afield. They converted an energetic Nordic means of personal transportation into an Alpine thrill, largely by mechanizing the remount, and established their own upmarket version of 'housey-housey'.[6] The emergence of winter sports and of the French Riviera and its jewel, the Casino at Monte Carlo, marked a turning point in the globalization of tourism.

Riviera and Alpine tourism indicate an upsurge in the reflexivity of tourist travel, the point at which tourism began to be consumed for its symbolic value, as a sign of affluence and cosmo-politanism. Signalling that one had holidayed could be accomplished by the possession of certain clothes worn outside the vacation, the ski jacket or the bikini, but more effectively by changes in the appearance of the body by allowing the sun to burn the skin (visible especially among the Anglo-Saxon, Celtic, Gallic, Teutonic and Scandinavian people of the North Atlantic rim) or even by having a broken limb encased in plaster. Such bodily mutilation could only legitimately be accomplished in particular climatic and environmental niches so tourists began to search the planet for duplicates. Importantly, these could not be achieved at British seaside resorts and their equivalents. In the post-Second World War period we therefore see a new combination of Riviera and Alpine tourism with the seaside in the form of the 'package holiday', an opportunity for the newly affluent working and middle classes to sample a Mediterranean or tropical climate without the uncertainties of the negotiation of travel arrangements with foreigners.

There is a sharp difference of opinion about whether this move constitutes or is the consequence of globalization in any absolute sense. For Urry (1990: 47–63) the movement of tourists between European countries or between say Japan and Thailand was indeed an internationalization of tourism that can be called globalized. For Turner and Ash (1975: 93–112), by contrast, it represents the creation of a 'pleasure periphery' that surrounded industrialized areas. Here the local culture was displaced in favour of tourist encapsulation where walled hotels offered familiar consumption patterns in a familiar language. North European societies created theirs in the Mediterranean; the pleasure periphery for North America is Florida, the Caribbean, Mexico and Hawaii; for Australia it is tropical Queensland, Bali and the South Pacific; for Japan and Korea it is South-East Asia; for Russia, the Black Sea; and for Brazil and Argentina it is Punta del Este in Uruguay. The argument here is that tourist operators will take punters just far enough to provide them with the prospect of the 'four Ss' of tourism (sun, sea, sand and sex) and no further because of transportation costs.

Turner and Ash's argument is more consistent with the globalization thesis because a more globalized form of tourism has emerged since the establishment of the pleasure periphery. It has several aspects. First, the package tour has achieved global extension. Mass tourism has moved beyond the pleasure

periphery in order to provide more exotic and 'risky' environments for the jaded tastes of metropolitan tourists. Europeans
and North Americans now swarm across the planet as one after
another destination becomes fashionable in Africa or Asia. For
example Bali, once the preserve of the colonial Dutch and nearby
Australians, is now knee-deep in Italians, French, Japanese and
Americans; the cruise up the Nile achieved a fleeting popularity
in the early 1980s and was then dropped; Sri Lanka was popular
with Germans and Scandinavians prior to its civil war; and anyone
flying from Australia to Britain on the 'Kangaroo route' via
Bangkok is likely to find the aircraft filled by package-holidaying
Britons weighed down by duty-free goods and bunches of orchids
as well as perhaps the odd STD. Second, the middle-class tourist
niche has been filled by 'new age travellers' and ecotourists.
These are independent travellers seeking out the last morsels of
authentic and exotic culture or of pristine environment. They
blaze the trail to the remaining untouched corners of the planet
for mass tourism and so, inevitably, consume the planet in the
fullest sense.

A third aspect of the recent globalization of tourism is conceivably the most interesting. This is the postmodernizing
declassification of tourist and non-tourist areas and the
accompanying declassification of cultures. This is most manifest
in a decline of the pleasure peripheries to follow the seaside
resorts. Kuta and Torremolinas are now regarded as *passé* as
Coney Island and Brighton. Moreover the 'funfairs' of the
pleasure periphery and their accompanying cultures, Disneyland
and the like, are now replicated in the heart of industrial
Europe and Japan where every town has a local theme park.
More importantly, there is no non-touristic space from which one
can escape. One can no more escape the tourist gaze by living in
Glasgow or Hobart or Guangzhou than by living in Orlando or
Cannes or Florence, perhaps less so because in the former one
is part of the object of attention while in the latter one is merely
incidental to the main event.

All of the above history indicates a rapid growth in international tourism in the second half of the twentieth century.
Indeed international tourism, measured by arrival from another
country, expanded seventeen-fold between 1950 and 1990 (*New
Internationalist* (245) 7/93). Most of this expansion has been European and North American (see Figure 6.1) but a significant
feature of the period we have previously identified as the phase

of accelerated globalization, from 1970 onwards, is the expansion of tourist arrivals outside Europe and the Americas. Tourism in the Asia-Pacific region is a central element in the transition outlined above. Figure 6.1 may also obscure the impact of tourism on individual societies outside the North Atlantic orbit. For example, in 1990 tourism receipts accounted for 67 per cent of Egypt's foreign exchange earnings, 55 per cent of Jamaica's, 43 per cent of Kenya's, and 30 per cent of Morocco's (*New Internationalist* (245) 7/93).

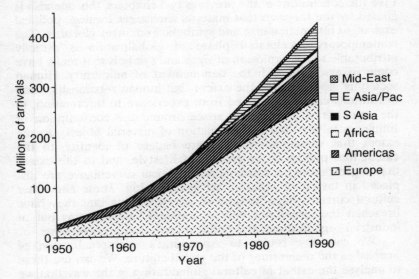

Figure 6.1 International tourist arrivals by region, 1950–90
Data source: *New Internationalist* (245) July 1993

The cultural impact of globalized tourism is multiple and complex but we can outline a few of the key dimensions here:

- the extent of globalized tourism indicates the extent to which tourists themselves conceptualize the world as a single place which is without internal geographical boundaries;
- globalization exposes tourists to cultural variation confirming the validity of local cultures and their differences;
- the objects of the tourist gaze are obliged to relativize

their activities, that is to compare and contrast it to the tastes of those that sightsee; in certain circumstances this may imply local cultural revival if only in simulated form;
- tourism extends consumer culture by redefining both human practices and the physical environment as commodities.

CONCLUSION: AN ECONOMY OF SIGNS AND SYMBOLS

Like the conclusions of the previous two chapters, this one also is guided by the theorem that material exchanges localize, political exchanges internationalize and symbolic exchanges globalize. The contemporary accelerated phase of globalization is directly attributable to the explosion of signs and symbols that many have come to associate with the denouement of modernity. Human society is globalizing to the extent that human relationships and institutions can be converted from experience to information, to the extent it is arranged in space around the consumption of simulacra rather than the production of material objects, to the extent that value-commitments are badges of identity, to the extent that politics is the pursuit of lifestyle, and to the extent that organizational constraints and political surveillance are displaced in favour of reflexive self-examination. These and other cultural currents have become so overwhelming that they have breached the levees not only of national value-systems but of industrial organizations and political-territorial arrangements.

We can now return to Appadurai's conceptualization of 'scapes' as the dimensions of the global culture. We can use these to analyse the extent of cultural globalization in the way that we have already done for political and economic globalization. This inventory is given in summary in Table 6.1. In each dimension globalization is highly advanced. Religious ideas must now be understood and often reinforced by fundamentalism in relation to the religions and the secularisms of all others. The commodification and marketing of religious ideas as a set of lifestyle choices is highly advanced and thus highly de-territorialized. Ethnoscapes are similarly relativized, dispersed and differentiated so that the modernist link between nation, state and territory appears permanently to have been disrupted. What we might call the econoscape, the pattern of exchange of valued items, is now dominated by the consumption of signs, images and information. Mediascapes are increasingly dominated by global production and distribution companies that offer common images across the globe. Under the heading of leisurescapes, or perhaps 'escapes', tourism is reaching its limits. Every corner of the globe is subject to its infestation and every person is a potential tourist and the potential object of tourism. Lash and Urry (1994) go so far as to project an 'end of tourism', a world so globalized that travel is a commonplace chore and where leisure and thrills are accessed through a video screen. This may not be such an immediate prospect as universal tourism but it is a clear possibility.

Table 6.1   An inventory of cultural globalization

Dimension	Ideal-typical pattern of globalization	Current state of affairs
Sacriscape	De-territorialized religious mosaic.	Relativization and fundamentalism.
Ethnoscape	De-territorialized cosmopolitanism and diversity.	Emergent infranationalism and supranationalism.
Econoscape	Consumption of simulations and representations.	Advanced dematerialization of commodities.
Mediascape	Global distribution of images and information.	De-regionalization of distribution of images and information.
Leisurescape	Universal tourism and the 'end of tourism'.	De-classification of subjects and objects.

7

The end of the world as we know it

It's a small world after all

popular jingle

These concluding comments are directed to three objectives: summarizing the general theme that links together the preceding chapters; considering the impact of globalization on sociology especially insofar as sociology can make a contribution to human welfare; and indicating the socio-spatial possibilities that might follow globalization.

A SUMMARY OF THE PROCESS OF GLOBALIZATION

In Chapter 1 we introduced a guiding theorem to provide a thematic link between the disparate elements of this, the most highly generalized of social processes. We can now give a summary account of its historical development. This summary will inevitably make sweeping and occasionally offensive claims, brushing aside the particularities of individual corners of the planet and the raggedness of social transformations in an effort to make generalized, perhaps overgeneralized sense out of daunting

complexity. The effort does not seek to deny the rich tapestry of
human experience, but if, as is widely recognized, globalization
is indeed occurring then it must by definition affect human
behaviour wherever it transpires.

Mobilizing the theoretical assumptions given in Chapter 1, we
have identified three arenas within which globalizing processes have
occurred, the economy, the polity and culture. These are set out in
the left column of Figure 7.1 through which this summary argument
can be traced. The relevant long-run general process that supports
globalization is specified under each of these in parentheses:
economies trend towards liberalization, that is freedom from command, constraint and status and class monopolization; polities trend
towards democratization, the deconcentration of power; and
culture towards universalization, the abstraction of values and
standards to a very high level of generality that will permit extreme
levels of cultural differentiation.

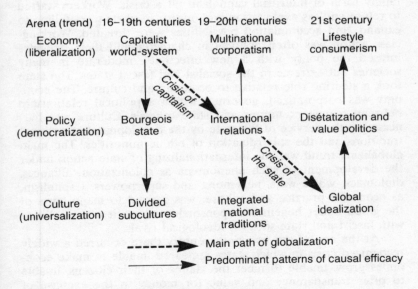

Figure 7.1 The path of globalization through time

These processes are carried forward through history by changes
in the relative efficacy of the three arenas. Historical time is
indicated by the column headings. This is largely a Western

European periodization, since Western European societies and their derivatives and mimics are the source and the leading edge of globalization. In the 'early modern' period between the six-teenth and nineteenth century the critical development was the emergence of capitalism. It was a set of material exchanges that proved highly effective in disrupting the traditionalistic ties of medieval society and it also penetrated and dominated politics and culture. Because such exchanges empowered a new capitalist class, it seriously weakened monarchies, either constitutionalizing them or rendering them ineffective, or it took over the state, reconstituting it as bourgeois and liberal. Equally cultures were divided and pervaded by ideology. The most important global links were those of trade, exploration and military adventure but, although they constituted a beginning they were relatively ineffective in establishing global integration.

At about the middle or end of the nineteenth century the family form of industrial capitalism hit a crisis. Workers started to refuse endless exploitation and misery, markets were failing to expand, and accumulation possibilities were threated. Working-class action was often political in character and their struggles infused the polity with a new effectivity, moderate in many societies but extreme in the socialist and fascist states. The state took a steering role relative to economy and culture. The econ-omy was corporatized, governed within a political relationship between managers, unions and state officials. Culture was har-nessed to the service of the state by the development of national traditions and the subordination of ethnic minorities. The main globalizing trend was the internationalizing of state action under the development of such phenomena as colonization, alliances, diplomacy, world wars, hegemons, and superpowers. Capitalism, as economic practice and culture, was carried to many parts of the globe under hegemonic sponsorship where it often collided with fascist and state-socialist ideological rivals.

At the end of the twentieth century there occurred a widely recognized crisis in which states appeared unable to make econ-omies grow, unable to meet the claims of their citizens, unable to offer transparency and value for money in the exercise of power, and unable to ensure a certain future for their populations. These populations have become more unwilling to surrender individual autonomy to superordinate organizations and have legitimated that claim by reference to universalized standards. This has involved an invocation of new political symbols and therefore a revitalization of cultural effectivity. The symbolic appeals centre on human rights, the planetary environment, liberal democratization, consumption rights, religious traditionalism, ethnic diversification, and cosmopolitanism, each of which institutionalizes globalizing practices and phenomenologies. Cultural action is now disrupting states, especially where they are most highly organized, and party politics is being disrupted by universalizing and diffuse social movements. Territorial boundaries are thus becoming more difficult to maintain. Meanwhile the economy is becoming dominated by lifestyle choices, both in terms of the displacement of production by consumption as the central economic activity and in terms of the diversification of possible occupational experiences. The economy is becoming symbolically mediated and reflexive which detaches it from locality.

GLOBALIZATION, SOCIOLOGY AND HUMAN EMANCIPATION

If globalization is a process that impels the development of cultural systems above all others, then the knowledge-system known as sociology cannot be immune from it. Indeed, a globalizing social world must oblige sociology reflexively to examine not only its theories but its scope as a community. There have been several clarion calls for a globalized sociology (e.g. Albrow 1990; Archer 1991; Moore 1966), each of which argues that both the content and the institutional arrangements of sociology should be expanded to match the onrush of social process.

Albrow (1990) gives the most systematic account of the development of sociology in the direction of globalization, arguing that it has developed through five stages of territorial reference. The stages are:

1 Universalism: here sociology was the science of humanity as a whole, seeking to discover general laws and principles applicable across time and space and that would thus provide a focus for a harmonious human unification; it is particularly associated with Saint-Simon, Comte, Spencer and Ward.

2 National sociologies: here sociology was harnessed to the project of nation-building especially insofar as it became a central discipline in some of the great metropolitan universities in Berlin, Paris, Chicago and so on; this was

the high classical period in sociology as practised by Weber, Durkheim and Mead, none of whom seemed to know much of each other.

3 Internationalization: French and German sociology had been disrupted by the world wars and the anthropological tradition was much stronger in Britain. However, American sociology prospered and indeed hosted European traditions introduced by the peripatetic Parsons and the refugee Schütz; American sociology became a model exporting an unlikely combination of Parsonsian grand theory and radical positivism to other parts of the world. The *International Sociological Association* (ISA) was founded in 1949 to assist the process.

4 Indigenization: this was a reaction to the hegemonic character of American sociology that began in the 'third world' in the 1970s but also extended to such peripheral societies as Australia and Canada. Indigenization also encompasses the revival of independent sociological traditions in Britain, France, Germany and Eastern Europe.

5 Globalization: the development of cross-national links between members of these independent sociological communities, particularly by means of the research committees of the ISA and specialized international conferences.

The claim for a globalized sociology is made against the claims of what Archer (1991: 135) calls the 'false universalism' of postmodernism. Postmodernism was an intellectual movement that affected sociology in the 1980s because it denied realism and totalizing theories in favour of the validity of individual opinion. Archer's characterization may be a little strong. Postmodernism might merely oblige sociologists not to privilege their own claims so that their: 'stories are part of a more general economy of discourse in which they must fight to find an audience and establish a salience in competition with other stories, and in the absence of guarantees' (Crook *et al.* 1992: 238). Globalization can offer an expansion of possibilities for sociology partly because it expands this marketplace for narratives, but not merely so. Globalization connects the local and national social structures, on which sociologists are already expert, within emerging supranational flows. Sociology is strategically, possibly uniquely placed to provide the local interpretations of globality which will be necessary if the inhabitants of the planet are to understand why their local and national political systems are approaching ineffectivity.

Indeed the provision of comprehensible accounts of globalization may not merely be a strategic but a moral imperative. As the leading critical social science, sociology has always claimed a central role in providing resources that will promote human emancipation. Sociologists, among others, deliver messages that cajole modern nation-states into egalitarian welfare provision. That provision is accomplished within the bundle of rights called citizenship, rights that protect the citizen from the exploitative ravages of the economy. Moreover, insofar as ordinary citizen-workers share in the decisions that control their lives they do so by electing representatives to national governments. This book tells us that the state, while not yet withered, is under threat and in decline. If the state disappears then so do citizenship and welfare rights and so too does liberal democracy. The inhabitants of the planet need to be able to devise and plan new means of social security and political expression that will protect them from impersonal flows of finance, taste and ideas. Sociology can at least advise them of the need for ingenuity in the construction of such arrangements.

This is not to suggest that the consequences for humanity of globalization are universally and entirely negative. A culture of taste and choice wins hands down over elitist imposts and class ideology in the emancipation stakes. And globalization encompasses such possibilities as the revival of previously oppressed nationalisms, genuine religious freedom based on genuine religious choice, the exposure of the great structures of economic and political domination to the winds of change, the emergence of a universal and feminist sisterhood from the confines of localized and nationalized patriarchies, and the possibility of migration to escape oppression. Sociology is also well placed to alert humanity to these possibilities.

POSTGLOBALIZATION

We might well end this particular sociological story on this optimistic note. However, we must finally consider whether there is any social possibility beyond globalization, other than a recessive social disintegration. To do so, let us consider a last characterization of the process. This book is about the relationship between social arrangements and space – globalization is defined, in the introductory chapter, as a reduction in the geographical constraints on social arrangements. In a globalized world the space within which social arrangements are made is the finite but unbounded and seamless surface of the planet. But society remains trapped in space precisely because the globe is indeed finite and because the existential link to space is the inescapable body. Even in a globalized world, our home is the planet.

The question now arises as to whether the space in which we live can be rendered infinite and whether social relations can be rendered independent of corporeal location. If we rule out mystical experiences of the 'out of body' type and religious claims about paradise we are left with one new and interesting possibility, virtual reality. Computers can already simulate a virtual space out of information. This 'cyberspace' bears no relationship to physical space and is limited only by the power of the computer(s) one uses. A highly simplified and finite version of such a space, tagged by familiar visual referents, is screened by many computer games – flight simulator type games, for example, are especially designed to simulate real space. It is now becoming increasingly possible to achieve direct sensual access to cyberspace by means of masking devices that fit screens to the eyes, speakerphones to the ears and control 'gloves' to the hands and feet. Using such a device it is possible to simulate an existence in cyberspace, that is, to simulate a body and a space that can be varied by design and thus by choice. Moreover to the extent that more than one person is connected to a network it is possible to set up shared experiences and therefore a social life in cyberspace. Real space loses any capacity to constrain social arrangements.

Not even in the science-fiction novels of William Gibson do 'cyberpunks' live out their entire lives in the 'net'. It is unlikely that virtual reality will ever offer anything other than a depthless version of reality. In any event the food is unlikely to be very nourishing and the sex anything but unsatisfying. Nevertheless it is possible to conceive of certain types of social relationship that could be liberated from spatial constraints entirely. Entertainment spectacles are a possibility but so also are business and governmental interactions. Perhaps a future World Congress of Sociology will be held not in Montreal or Madrid but in a cyberspace that is no place.

Notes

1 A WORLD OF DIFFERENCE

[1] Without becoming too pedantic this word has at least three meanings: spherical, total/universal, and world-wide. It is the third of these that is relevant here.

[2] There are obviously certain kinship relationships which are immune to globalizing effects. However, geographically distant spousal relationships are already becoming more common.

[3] Some examples of these are set out in Table 1. Column 1 indicates widespread agreement that society has a differentiated economic arena that is concerned with the production of material items and that generates socio-economic inequalities.

Column 2 indicates a similar measure of agreement that there is a differentiated political, governmental or state arena that focuses on authoritative decision-making, coordination and goal attainment. Most authors agree that there is at least a third and often a fourth region but there is less than widespread agreement on the constitution of that region. Some authors see it as emotional and expressive (Connell, Habermas), others as normative and value-oriented (Parsons, Etzioni), while still others view the region as ideological (Althusser, Mann). Yet they are all in the region of culture in which human orientations are shared and mediated through symbols.

Author	1	2	3
Hegel	Civil society	State	Family/religion
Gramsci	Economy	State	Civil society
Marshall	Economic rights	Political rights	Civil rights
Parsons	Economy	Polity	Community/fiduciary
Althusser	Economic base	State	Ideology
Bell	Techno-economic	Political	Cultural
Etzioni	Utilitarian	Coercive	Normative
Connell	Labour	Power	Cathexis
Habermas 1	Work	Power	Knowledge
Habermas 2	Economy	Polity	Public/private lifeworld
Mann	Economic power	Political/military power	Ideological power
Wright	Property	Organizational assets	Credentials

2 WHAT ON EARTH IS HAPPENING?: PRECURSOR THEORIES

[1] This sentence shamelessly mixes several metaphors, most of which are equally shamelessly lifted from the works of others, particularly of course, Levy's (1966) 'modernization as the universal solvent', Giddens' (1990) 'juggernaut of modernity' and the reverse aviation of Benjamin's 'angel of history' (1973: 259–60).

[2] While many modernization theorists insist on a logic of choice, several accept that modernization spreads through the impositions of political or economic imperialism.

[3] For a more comprehensive but nevertheless short account of Parsons' theory of evolution, see Waters (1994: 305–7).

[4] I first heard this metaphor used by Ronald Dore in Moncton N.B. Canada in 1975.

[5] A Portuguese term which literally means 'buyer'. A comprador elite or bourgeoisie merely buys and sells, it does not produce anything.

[6] Indeed the discipline of International Relations is currently engaged in a paralysing debate between so-called 'realists' who argue that the state is the site of real power and so-called 'modernists' who argue more or less in favour of globalization.

[7] 'International Relations' (first letters upper case) will indicate the subdiscipline. The term without the upper case indicates the subject matter studied within the subdiscipline.

[8] Burton calls this model a 'billiard-ball model'. However, billiards is a game played with three balls of two colours. Snooker, with its differentiation of colours and points values and greater complexity of interaction, might be a better metaphor. It is also a far superior game.

[9] A similar but more recent argument is made by Luard (1990) although it appears, at first glance, to be more committed to a globalization thesis. National societies, he argues, are becoming attenuated by internal divisions and conflicts, not merely between minority nationalities but by religious and ideological differences and class divisions. At the same time the multiplication of inter-state relationships supports the view that we should recognize that international society is almost equally as important. However, Luard appears to remain not entirely convinced by his own claims. The list of key characteristics given for international society (1990: 6–10) is a list of the things that it lacks: it lacks centralized authority, a formal structure of relationships, a sense of communal solidarity, a sense of obligation to a legitimate order, and a consensus on common values. Nevertheless, Luard hesitantly suggests, it is a society 'of a kind'. The kind of society he specifies almost returns us to early theories of international relations. International society encompasses both relations between states and transnational practices between non-state actors. However: 'The relationships which individuals can undertake across frontiers depend on the understandings and agreements reached between governments. And the general character of international society at any one time, including its characteristic 'ideology', is thus determined by the actions and decisions of states more than by those of individuals or groups' (1990: 5).

[10] A similar and equally influential version of the argument is given by Keohane and Nye (1973). However, their analysis matches Rosenau's so closely that it would add little to review both.

[11] This technological version of post-industrialization is inconsistent with Bell's original formulation (1976) which insists on the importance of service production and of intellectual technology.

[12] Gilpin has a technological cake in the oven to go along with the etatist one he is eating and the economic one he is keeping:

> Improvements in communications and transportation that reduce the cost of conducting business have encouraged the integration of once isolated markets into an expanding global interdependence. From the innovation of oceangoing sailing ships to contemporary information-processing systems, technological advances have been an almost inexorable force for uniting the world economy.
>
> (1987: 82)

[13] The term 'global village' was actually introduced apparently accidentally in the introduction to an earlier anthology: 'Postliterate man's electronic media contract the world to a village or tribe where everything happens to everyone at the same time: everyone knows about, and therefore participates in, everything that is happening the minute it happens. Television gives this quality of simultaneity to events in the global village' (Carpenter and McLuhan 1970: xi). The term achieved wide currency and appeal. In the second edition of the *OED* it occupies much more space than 'globalization' (*OED* 1989 *s.v.* global village).

3 BRAVE NEW WORLDS: RECENT THEORIES

[1] McGrew (1992a: 66) claims that two authors, Giddens and Harvey, have made significant contributions to the theorization of globalization. He identifies Robertson as a member of what he calls the Giddens' 'multicausal school' of globalization theory. This may give a misleading impression of the provenance of the concept. Robertson's own view of Giddens' work (1992: 138–45) sees it as adding little to

globalization theory. It is, for him, merely 'an updated and overly abstracted version of the convergence thesis' (1992: 145). It is certainly the case that Giddens did not use the term 'globalization' until long after Robertson had it in print. Robertson himself says: 'Giddens comes, rather late, to the theme of globalization' (1992: 141).

[2] The theoretical argument of this book, especially insofar as it relates to the effects of a symbolic economy on globalization, are broadly consistent with Lash and Urry. It is not referenced against them because it was written before their book was published.

[3] As might be gathered from the quotations given here, Beck's book *Risk Society* (1992) was originally published in German in 1986. He wrote it at a time of high consciousness of ecological threats from acid rain and not long after the Chernobyl nuclear meltdown that scattered radioactivity over much of north-western Europe. Global politics were still gripped by a superpower duopoly that provided the very real threat of a global nuclear holocaust.

[4] We think, for example, of London and New York as being 'closer' by Concorde than by Boeing 747. Astrophysics has long since gone all the way on this one, measuring distances between stars in 'light years'.

[5] This might be illustrated by the phenomenological disjunctions that are now appearing between real time and computed time, between physical space and cyberspace, and between reality and virtual reality. In some senses the computer simulations of time, space and reality, that curve around the physical counterpart, might be held phenomenologically to be 'more real' (for further discussion, see Chapter 7).

4 WORLD CLASS PRODUCTION: ECONOMIC GLOBALIZATION

[1] In Figure 4.1 and throughout this chapter the following abbreviations apply: CPEs = Centrally Planned Economies (usually the former USSR, People's Republic of China, former post-war socialist states of Eastern Europe); DMEs = Democratic Market Economies (usually North America, Japan, Western Europe, Australasia); EU = European Union (including its predecessors EC (European

Communities); EEC (European Economic Community; data often exclude the UK), ECSC (European Coal and Steel Community); data prior to 1960 are often for (W) Germany and France only); LDCs = Less Developed Countries (usually any country not in any other group); NICs = Newly Industrializing Countries (usually the Asian dragons, plus Brazil, Chile and Mexico).

[2] Entering an agreement in which the allied firms sell each other's products under their own brand name. Possibly the best-known example is the rebadging of Honda cars produced in Britain as 'Rovers'.

[3] Fordism was indeed paradigmatic and idealized rather than generalized. It never accounted for more than 10 per cent of manufacturing labour, even in the USA (Crook *et al.* 1992: 172).

[4] Crook *et al.* (1992) argue that hyperdifferentiation implies dedifferentiation.

[5] The advantages and the branch-plant effect are most apparent in the motor vehicle industry. For example, in 1982 Toyota could produce 56 cars per employee per year, whereas Ford could produce only 12. During the 1980s Toyota established major manufacturing capacity in Australia, Canada, Britain and the USA, often in alliance with GM (Wilkinson *et al.* 1992).

[6] This section relies on Crook *et al.* (1992: 178–92).

[7] There is some variation in opinion about the extent of diffusion of QCCs. Swyngedouw (1987: 493) says that currently there are 100,000 operational in Japan, that is, in 71 per cent of all firms and in 91 per cent of firms with more than 10,000 workers. Mathews (1989: 81) says that there are about a million QCCs in Japan and that 100,000 had been formed in Southeast Asia during the previous ten years. Although the growth of QCCs is doubtless exponential it is unlikely to have increased tenfold in two years, even in Japan.

[8] In Japan 54 per cent of firms with less than 300 employees are subcontractors; 25 per cent of all such firms subcontract to only one core firm (Swyndgedouw 1987: 496).

[9] Wages of workers in Japanese firms with less than 100 employees average 62 per cent of those in firms with more than 500 employees, while those in firms with 100–500 employees average 81 per cent of the wages of those in large firms (Swyngedouw 1987: 497).

[10] In the new culturalist language, a Fordist organization has 'weak' culture because it relies for control on technology rather than commitment. Sociologically, however, Fordism was at least as effective in cultural terms as the new paradigm.

[11] Although Soros has been mentioned widely in academic circles as an example of a capitalist who can move governments, he did so because he speculated against their currencies and not because he ruled or controlled them. Soros cannot be regarded as a traditional industrial capitalist located in a class struggle with a proletariat. He is simply a market speculator on a grand scale.

5 EARTHLY POWERS: POLITICAL GLOBALIZATION

[1] This is enshrined in two legal principles: 'immunity from jurisdiction' – 'no state can be sued in courts of another state for acts performed in its sovereign capacity'; and 'immunity of state agencies' – 'should an individual break the law of another state while acting as an agent of his country of origin and be brought before that state's courts, he is not held "guilty" because he did not act as a private individual but as the representative of the state' (Cassese in Held 1991: 218).

[2] For a summary of part of Beck's argument, see Chapter 2 of this book.

[3] The *pan-ic* (i.e. totalizing) status of AIDS is critical to the present argument. Unlike bubonic plague it is not merely *pandemic*. Victims and therapists alike view the disease as an aspect of a world-wide human community in a way that medieval sufferers from bubonic plague probably rarely did.

[4] The extent to which states have surrendered sovereignty can be confirmed by the existence of a speciality in policy analysis known as Global Policy Studies. See the special issues on the topic of the *International Political Science Review* 11(3): July 1990 and the *Journal of Peace Research* 27(2): May 1990.

[5] The growth of IGOs and INGOs may have surprised even the most expert observers. In 1983 Archer estimated that by the turn of the 21st century IGOs would remain at about 300 and INGOs might number 9,600 (1983: 171). By 1992

the respective figures were 3,188 and 14,733 (UIA 1992: 1671).

[6] Fukuyama argues against Islamic theocracy as a serious challenge to liberal democracy on the grounds that it applies only in societies that have long been religiously and culturally Moslem. It cannot expand beyond these boundaries and is active and virulent partly because many of its adherents are tempted by liberal democracy (1992: 45–6).

6 THE NEW WORLD CHAOS: CULTURAL GLOBALIZATION

[1] *The Economist* explains that: 'many Japanese prefer to see the West without having to leave Japan. The real West is too far, too dangerous and, quite honestly, too foreign' (22–28/1/94).

[2] The images created by the Hollywood movie industry, for example, doubtless represented an 'America of the desire' that the central European Jewish emigrés who ran it aspired to.

[3] Monash University in Melbourne which markets its programmes in standardized packages throughout Asia is known colloquially and offensively as McMonash.

[4] A measure of the general acceptance of global imagery might be the title of the most popular manual for the Internet, *The Whole Internet User's Guide and Catalog* (Krol 1992) that is based on the title of a much earlier manual for environmentally friendly consumption *The Whole Earth Catalog*.

[5] Cook took his first group to America in 1866, he took 20,000 people to the Paris exhibition in 1867, and he organized his first round-the-world tour in 1872. Globalization had apparently proceeded apace because he was able to boast that: 'This going round the world is a very easy and almost imperceptible business' (Turner and Ash 1975: 55–6).

[6] An English working-class name for a numbers gambling game known in other versions as 'bingo', 'lotto' or 'keno'.

References

Albrow, M. (1990) 'Introduction' in M. Albrow and E. King (eds) *Globalization, Knowledge and Society*, London: Sage.

Amin, S. (1980) *Class and Nation*, New York: Monthly Review.

Anderson, B. (1983) *Imagined Communities*, London: Verso.

Anderson, M. (1984) *Madison Avenue in Asia*, Cranbury: Associated University Press.

Appadurai, A. (1990) 'Disjuncture and Difference in the Global Cultural Economy' in M. Featherstone (ed.) *Global Culture*, London: Sage: 295–310.

Archer, C. (1983) *International Organizations*, London: Allen & Unwin.

Archer, M. (1990) 'Theory, Culture and Post-Industrial Society' in M. Featherstone (ed.) *Global Culture*, London: Sage: 97–120.

Archer, M. (1991) 'Sociology for One World: Unity and Diversity' *International Sociology* 6(2): 131–47.

Arnason, J. (1990) 'Nationalism, Globalization and Modernity' in M. Featherstone (ed.) *Global Culture*, London: Sage: 207–36.

Barker, E. (1991) 'The Whole World in His Hand?' in R. Robertson and W. Garrett (eds) *Religion and Global Order*, New York: Paragon: 201–20.

Barraclough, G. (ed.) (1978) *The Times Atlas of World History*, London: Times.

Baudrillard, J. (1988) *Selected Writings*, Stanford: Stanford University Press.

Beck, U. (1992) *Risk Society*, London: Sage.

Bell, D. (1976) *The Coming of Post-Industrial Society*, New York: Basic.

Bell, D. (1979) *The Cultural Contradictions of Capitalism* (2nd edn), London: Heinemann.

Bell, D. (1987) 'The World and the United States in 2013' *Daedalus* 116(3): 1–30.

Benjamin, W. (1973) *Illuminations*, London: Fontana.

Beyer, P. (1990) 'Privatization and the Public Influence of Religion in Global Society' in M. Featherstone (ed.) *Global Culture*, London: Sage: 373–96.

Brubaker, R. (1984) *The Limits of Rationality*, London: Allen & Unwin.

Bull, H. (1977) *The Anarchical Society*, New York: Columbia University Press.

Burton, J. (1972) *World Society*, Cambridge: Cambridge University Press.

Carpenter, E. and M. McLuhan (eds) (1970) *Explorations in Communication*, London: Cape

Cassese, A. (1991) 'Violence, War and the Rule of Law' in D. Held (ed.) *Political Theory Today*, Cambridge: Polity: 255–75.

Champagne, D. (1992) 'Transocietal [sic] Cultural Exchange within the World Economic and Political System' in P. Colomy (ed.) *The Dynamics of Social Systems*, London: Sage: 120–53.

Cockroft, J., A. Frank and D. Johnson (1972) *Dependence and Underdevelopment*, Garden City: Anchor.

Cohen, R. (1987) *The New Helots*, Aldershot: Avebury.

Crook, S., J. Pakulski and M. Waters (1992) *Postmodernization*, London: Sage.

Dohse, K., U. Jürgens and T. Malsch (1985) 'From "Fordism" to "Toyotism"? The Social Organization of the Japanese Automobile Industry' *Politics & Society*, 14(2): 115–46.

Dore, R. (1989) 'Where Are We Going Now?' *Work, Employment and Society* 14(2): 425–46.

Duke, J. and B. Johnson (1989) 'Religious Transformation and Social Conditions' in W Swatos (ed.) *Religious Politics in Global Perspective*, New York: Greenwood: 75–110.

Dunning, J. (1993) *Multinational Enterprises in a Global Economy*, Wokingham: Addison-Wesley.

Durkheim, E. (1984 [1895]) *The Division of Labour in Society*, Basingstoke: Macmillan.

Emmott, B. (1993) 'Everybody's Favourite Monsters' *The Economist* 27/3 (supplement).

Featherstone, M. (ed.) (1990) *Global Culture*, London: Sage.

Featherstone, M. (1991) *Consumer Culture and Postmodernism*, London: Sage.

Foster, R. (1991) 'Making National Cultures in the Global Ecumene' *Annual Review of Anthropology* 20: 235–60.

Frank, A. (1971) *Capitalism and Underdevelopment in Latin America* (revised edn.), Harmondsworth: Penguin.

Friedman, J. (1990) 'Being in the World: Globalization and Localization' in M. Featherstone (ed.) *Global Culture*, London: Sage: 311–28.

Fröbel, F., J. Heinrichs and O. Kreye (1980) *The New International Division of Labour*, Cambridge: Cambridge University Press.

Fukuyama, F. (1992) *The End of History and the Last Man*, London: Hamish Hamilton.

Giddens, A. (1981) *A Contemporary Critique of Historical Materialism*, London: Macmillan.

Giddens, A. (1985) *The Nation-State and Violence*, Cambridge: Polity.

Giddens, A. (1990) *The Consequences of Modernity*, Cambridge: Polity.

Giddens, A. (1991) *Modernity and Self-Identity*, Cambridge: Polity.

Gilpin, R. (1987) *The Political Economy of International Relations*, Princeton: Princeton University Press.

Gleich, J. (1987) *Chaos*, London: Cardinal.

Gordon, D. (1988) 'The Global Economy: New Edifice or Crumbling Foundation?' *New Left Review* (168): 24–64.

Haddon, J. (1991) 'The Globalization of American Televangelism' in R. Robertson and W. Garrett (eds) *Religion and Global Order*, New York: Paragon: 221–44.

Hall, N. (ed.) (1992a) *The New Scientist Guide to Chaos*, Harmondsworth: Penguin.

Hall, S. (1992b) 'The Question of Cultural Identity' in S. Hall, D. Held and T. McGrew (eds) *Modernity and its Futures*, Cambridge: Polity: 274–316.

Harvey, D. (1989) *The Condition of Postmodernity*, Oxford: Blackwell.

Held, D. (1991) 'Democracy and the Global System' in D. Held (ed.) *Political Theory Today*, Cambridge: Polity: 197–235.

Hobsbawm, E. (1992) *Nations and Nationalism since 1780* (2nd edn.), Cambridge: Cambridge University Press.

Hook, G. and M. Weiner (1992) *The Internationalization of Japan*, London: Routledge.

Hopkins, T. and I. Wallerstein (eds) (1980) *Processes of the World-System*, Beverly Hills: Sage.

Hopkins, T. and I. Wallerstein (eds) (1982) *World-Systems Analysis*, Beverly Hills: Sage.

Hoskins, C. and R. Mirus (1988) 'Reasons for the US Dominance of the International Trade in Television Programs' *Media, Culture and Society* 10: 499–515.

Huntington, S. (1991) *The Third Wave*, Norman: Oklahoma University Press.

Inglehart, R. (1990) *Culture Shift in Advanced Industrial Society*, Princeton: Princeton University Press.

Kavolis, V. (1988) 'Contemporary Moral Cultures and "the Return of the Sacred" ' *Sociological Analysis* 49(3): 203–16.

Keohane, R. and J. Nye (eds) (1973) *Transnational Relations and World Politics*, Cambridge: Harvard University Press.

Kerr, C., J. Dunlop, F. Harbison and Myers, C. (1973) *Industrialism and Industrial Man*, Harmondsworth: Penguin.

King, A. (1990a) 'Architecture, Capital and the Globalization of Culture' in M. Featherstone (ed.) *Global Culture*, London: Sage: 397–411.

King, A. (1990b) *Global Cities*, London: Routledge.

Krol, E. (1992) *The Whole Internet*, Sebastapol: O'Reilly.

Kuttner, R. (1991) *The End of Laissez-Faire*, New York: Knopf.

Lash, S. and J. Urry (1987) *The End of Organized Capitalism*, Cambridge: Polity.

Lash, S. and J. Urry (1994) *Economies of Signs and Space*, London: Sage.

Lechner, F. (1989) 'Cultural Aspects of the Modern World-System' in W Swatos (ed.) *Religious Politics in Global and Comparative Perspective*, New York: Greenwood: 11–28.

Lechner, F. (1990) 'Fundamentalism Revisited' in T. Robbins and D. Anthony *In Gods We Trust*, New Brunswick: Transaction.

Lechner, F. (1991) 'Religion, Law and Global Order' in R.

Robertson and W. Garrett (eds) *Religion and Global Order*, New York: Paragon: 263–80.

Lechner, F. (1992) 'Against Modernity: Antimodernism in Global Perspective' in P. Colomy (ed.) *The Dynamics of Social Systems*, London: Sage: 72–92.

Lenin, V. (1939) *Imperialism*, New York: International.

Levitt, T. (1983) 'The Globalization of Markets' *Harvard Business Review* 83(3): 92–102.

Levy, M. (1966) *Modernization and the Structure of Societies*, Princeton: Princeton University Press.

Long, T. (1991) 'Old Testament Universalism' in R. Robertson and W. Garrett (eds) *Religion and Global Order*, New York: Paragon: 19–34.

Lovelock, J. (1987) *Gaia*, Oxford: Oxford University Press.

Luard, E. (1990) *International Society*, Basingstoke: Macmillan.

Lyotard, J-F. (1984) *The Postmodern Condition*, Manchester: Manchester University Press.

McEvedy, C. and R. Jones (1978) *Atlas of World Population History*, Harmondsworth: Penguin.

McGrew, A. (1992a) 'A Global Society?' in S. Hall, D. Held and T. McGrew (eds) *Modernity and its Futures*, Cambridge: Polity: 62–113.

McGrew, A. (1992b) 'Conceptualizing Global Politics' in A. McGrew, P. Lewis *et al. Global Politics*, Cambridge: Polity: 1–29.

McLuhan, M. (1964) *Understanding Media*, London: Routledge.

McLuhan, M. and Q. Fiore (1967) *The Medium is the Massage*, London: Allen Lane.

McLuhan, M. and Q. Fiore (1968) *War and Peace in the Global Village*, New York: Bantam.

Marceau, J. (ed.) (1992) *Reworking the World*, Berlin: De Gruyter.

Marshall, T. (1973) *Class, Citizenship and Social Development*, Westport: Greenwood.

Marx, K. (1977) *Selected Writings*, Oxford: Oxford University Press.

Mathews, J. (1984) *Tools of Change*, Sydney: Pluto.

Meadows, D., D. Meadows, J. Randers and W. Behrens (1976) *The Limits to Growth*, Scarborough: Signet.

Moore, W. (1966) 'Global Sociology: The World as a Singular System' *American Journal of Sociology* 71(5): 475–82.

Mowlana, H. (1985) *International Flow of Information: A Global Report and Analysis*, Paris: UNESCO.

Muldoon, J. (1991) 'The Conquest of the Americas: the Spanish Search for Global Order' in R. Robertson and W. Garrett (eds) *Religion and Global Order*, New York: Paragon: 65–86.

Nettl, J. and R. Robertson (1968) *International Systems and the Modernization of Societies*, London: Faber.

OECD [Organization for Economic Co-operation and Development] (1987) *Interdependence and Co-operation in Tomorrow's World*, OECD: Paris.

OECD (1992) *Globalisation of Industrial Activities*, OECD: Paris.

O'Neill, J. (1990) 'AIDS as a Globalizing Panic' in M. Featherstone (ed.) *Global Culture*, London: Sage: 329–42.

Parsons, T. (1964) 'Evolutionary Universals in Society' *American Sociological Review* 29: 339–57.

Parsons, T. (1966) *Societies*, Englewood Cliffs: Prentice-Hall.

Parsons, T. (1977) *The Evolution of Societies*, Englewood Cliffs: Prentice-Hall.

Parsons, T. and N. Smelser (1968) *Economy and Society*, London: Routledge.

Ritzer, G. (1993) *The McDonaldization of Society*, Thousand Oaks: Pine Forge.

Robertson, R. (1983) 'Interpreting Globality' in R. Robertson *World Realities and International Studies*, Glenside: Pennsylvania Council on International Education.

Robertson, R. (1985) 'The Relativization of Societies: Modern Religion and Globalization' in T. Robbins, W. Shepherd and J. McBride (eds) *Cults, Culture and the Law*, Chicago: Scholars.

Robertson, R. (1992) *Globalization*, London: Sage.

Robertson, R. and Garrett, W. (eds) *Religion and Global Order*, New York: Paragon.

Rosenau, J. (1980) *The Study of Global Interdependence*, New York: Nichols.

Rosenau, J. (1990) *Turbulence in World Politics*, Princeton: Princeton University Press.

Saint-Simon, H. (1975 [1802–25]) *Selected Writings on Science, Industry and Social Organisation*, London: Croom Helm.

Shields, R. (1991) *Places on the Margin*, London: Routledge.

Shupe, A. (1991) 'Globalization versus Religious Nativism: Japan's Soka Gakkai in the World Arena' in R. Robertson and

W. Garrett (eds) *Religion and Global Order*, New York: Paragon: 183–200.

Sklair, L. (1991) *Sociology of the Global System*, Hemel Hempstead: Harvester Wheatsheaf.

Smart, B. (1993) *Postmodernity*, London: Routledge.

Strange, J. (1991) 'Two Aspects of the Development of Universalism in Christianity' in R. Robertson and W. Garrett (eds) *Religion and Global Order*, New York: Paragon: 35–46.

Swyngedouw, E. (1987) 'Social Innovation, Product Organization and Spatial Development: the Case of Japanese Manufacturing' *Revue d'Economie Régionale et Urbaine* 3: 487–510.

Thompson, P. and D. McHugh (1990) *Work Organisations*, Basingstoke: Macmillan.

Turner, B. (1990) 'The Two Faces of Sociology: Global or National?' in M. Featherstone (ed.) *Global Culture*, London: Sage: 343–58.

Turner, B. (1991) 'Politics and Culture in Islamic Globalism' in R. Robertson and W. Garrett (eds) *Religion and Global Order*, New York: Paragon: 161–82.

Turner, L. and J. Ash (1975) *The Golden Hordes*, London: Constable.

UIA [Union of International Associations] (1992) *Yearbook of International Organizations 1992/3*, Munich: Saur.

Urry, J. (1990) *The Tourist Gaze*, London: Sage.

Van der Pijl, K. (1989) 'The International Level' in T. Bottomore and R. Brym (eds) *The Capitalist Class*, Hemel Hempstead: Harvester Wheatsheaf: 237–66.

Vogler, J. (1992) 'Regimes and the Global Commons' in A. McGrew and P. Lewis *et al. Global Politics*, Cambridge: Polity: 118–37.

Wallerstein, I. (1974) *The Modern World-System*, New York: Academic.

Wallerstein, I. (1980) *The Modern World-System II*, New York: Academic.

Wallerstein, I. (1990) 'Culture as the Ideological Battleground of the Modern World-System' in M. Featherstone (ed.) *Global Culture*, London: Sage: 31–56.

Walters, R. and D. Blake (1992) *The Politics of Global Economic Relations*, Englewood Cliffs: Prentice-Hall.

Waters, M. (1994) *Modern Sociological Theory*, London: Sage.

Weber, M. (1978) *Economy and Society*, Berkeley: University of California Press.

Wilkinson, B., J. Morris and N. Oliver (1992) 'Japanizing the World: the Case of Toyota' in J. Marceau (ed.) *Reworking the World*, Berlin: De Gruyter: 133–50.

Index